4 25

Australia

by Bruce Brander, Mary Ann Harrell, and Hector Holthouse

Foreword by Gilbert M. Grosvenor, Associate Editor,
National Geographic Magazine

Prepared by National Geographic Special Publications Division
Robert L. Breeden, Chief

National Geographic Society, Washington, D. C.
Melvin M. Payne, President
Melville Bell Grosvenor, Editor-in-Chief
Frederick G. Vosburgh, Editor

AUSTRALIA

AUSTRALIA

BY BRUCE BRANDER, MARY ANN
HARRELL, AND HECTOR HOLTHOUSE

Published by
THE NATIONAL GEOGRAPHIC SOCIETY
MELVIN M. PAYNE, *President*
MELVILLE BELL GROSVENOR,
   Editor-in-Chief
FREDERICK G. VOSBURGH, *Editor*
GILBERT M. GROSVENOR, *Executive
   Editor for this Series*

Prepared by
THE SPECIAL PUBLICATIONS DIVISION
ROBERT L. BREEDEN, *Editor*
DONALD J. CRUMP, *Associate Editor*
PHILIP B. SILCOTT, *Assistant Editor*
HOWELL WALKER, *Consulting Editor*
LINDA M. SEEMAN, *Research*
TEE LOFTIN SNELL, PEGGY WINSTON,
   Research Assistants
RONALD M. FISHER, CYNTHIA RAMSAY,
   TEE LOFTIN SNELL, GERALD S.
   SNYDER, *Picture Legends*
MARY ANN HARRELL, *Style*
LUBA BALKO, MARGARET S. DEAN,
   CAROL OAKES, URSULA ROTH,
   BARBARA WALKER, *Editorial Assistants*

Illustrations and Design
DAVID R. BRIDGE, *Picture Editor*
JOSEPH A. TANEY, *Art Director*
JOSEPHINE B. BOLT, *Assistant Art
   Director*

Production and Printing
ROBERT W. MESSER, *Production*
JAMES R. WHITNEY, *Engraving and
   Printing*
JOHN R. METCALFE, *Assistant,
   Engraving and Printing*
DOROTHY CORSON, ANNE McCAIN,
   Index

*Scurrying Merinos clear a path for grazier
Brian Thompson on his 9,978-acre sheep
station in New South Wales. Overleaf: National symbols, the kangaroo and emu domi-
nate the Commonwealth's coat of arms. The
shield bears emblems of the six states. Page
one: Duckbill platypus, an egg-laying mam-
mal found only in Australia, reaches a length
of one and a half to two feet. Much of the
country's diverse fauna exists nowhere else.*

NATIONAL GEOGRAPHIC PHOTOGRAPHER WINFIELD PARKS (RIGHT)
AND ARTISTS RICHARD SCHLECHT (OVERLEAF) AND JAY H.
MATTERNES (PAGE ONE); ROUTE MAPS, GEOGRAPHIC ART DIVISION

Foreword

LIKE PRACTICALLY EVERYONE who visits Australia, I found myself quickly captivated by this immense and compelling country. Its greatest appeal, to me, is its people—their spirit and informal way of living; for others it might well be the sophisticated cities, the Great Barrier Reef, the half-explored outback that hides a treasure of mineral wealth, or perhaps simply the rich, gently rolling farmlands.

Whatever one's preference, it is vividly presented in the 220 colorful and informative pages of this book, undertaken by the Society in response to its members' many expressions of interest in Australia.

I first arrived in Australia late one night at the Sydney airport with my wife Donna—and within minutes formed my most memorable Australian friendship. Tired from hours of jet travel, Donna and I watched the last available taxi disappear down a rain-swept street. At that grim moment a private car pulled up, and the driver called to us with cheerful Aussie informality. He had seen our predicament and insisted on taking us to our hotel—and he expressed keen disappointment that we could not accept an invitation to stay in his own home. To this day we rekindle our friendship through Christmas greeting cards.

All during our travels, we experienced the same courtesy. And proud Australians enjoyed sharing their magnificent continent with us. Inevitably, we compared their country with ours. The tropical beauty of the Reef recalled the Straits of Florida; rugged mountains reminded us of New England; from the air Sydney resembled the San Francisco Bay area.

Broad reaches of dry plain, like parts of our West, hold great potential, needing only irrigation to produce enough food for millions of people. Mineral discoveries are swelling the country's wealth, as they have in the United States. Indeed, Australia—the world's only country commanding an entire continent—boasts natural riches rivaled by few nations.

Thoughtful Australians are quick to explain that lodes of ore alone do not account for the present boom. "Our prosperity," they say, "comes from a fact so obvious that it's easily overlooked, the fact that this is a politically stable country." Australia is one of the world's most successful democracies —heir to many generations' experience in the Old World, yet fortunate in a sense of youth, comparatively unencumbered by time and the weight of tradition. The nation has heritage enough to establish its own unmistakable identity, yet not enough to hold the country back.

Americans are taking more and more interest in Australia. I have found many who agree with Donna and me—that Australians are closer to us than any other people, in personality and spirit. Yet we recognize their distinctive character at once, in their vigorous idiom, their stimulating and bruising sports, their literature and painting, their beer and their suntans. Australians are like ... Australians. I can think of no higher compliment.

GILBERT M. GROSVENOR

Contents

Foreword   5

1   The Island Continent: a Young Nation, an Old Land   9

2   On the Boomerang Coast, Home to Most Australians   21

3   Melbourne, Canberra, and Men Who Capture Rivers   45

4   Sydney, Cradle of a Country; Bathurst and Merino Wool   69

5   Queensland: Gold in the Hills and Gold Along the Beach   97

6   Air Bus on a 'Stations Run' From Cairns Into the Outback   121

7   The West: Mountains of Iron, Islands of Oil   145

8   Perth, Glints of Gold, and a Treeless Plain   169

9   The Center: Journey Into Alice's Wonderland   193

Index   216

Service! Children practice tennis strokes in a suburb of Canberra, the federal capital.
Australians have won the coveted Davis Cup 15 times since World War II.

1

The Island Continent:
A Young Nation, an Old Land

BRUCE BRANDER

"PUT THE RUDDER HARD RIGHT." The captain spoke quietly in his wheel-house. The helmsman, standing with feet apart for steadiness in the center of the bridge, rotated the wheel several spokes at a time. More than 20,000 tons of ocean liner began to come around. At the radar screen, I felt the deck throb with more engine vibration than usual. We rolled a little. Then Australia, vaguely visible for the past hour or so, lay dead ahead.

Capt. Charles Wright aimed binoculars from a rectangular window. He looked over the foredeck and the sea beyond, to the cliff-walled Sydney Harbour entrance. "How are you heading now?"

"Three-one-zero, sir."

"Steady as she goes," the captain ordered. Steady on a compass course of 310 degrees, the sleek white liner *Mariposa* glided toward the last horizon on a Pacific Ocean voyage 7,254 miles long.

High above us, breaking from a solid sheet of cloud, a jet shot like a black dart toward the continent. My co-author Mary Ann Harrell of the Geographic staff would arrive aboard a giant aircraft. Her plane would vault the whole Pacific in a few great bounds. Leaping off California to Hawaii, the airliner would hurtle the Equator to Auckland, New Zealand, hop again, and then, after less than a day's time at 600 miles an hour, enter a 120-mile descent to Sydney.

On vacation aboard the *Mariposa,* I had taken a leisurely three weeks

Storm-driven surf booms among offshore rocks on the southeast coast of Australia, dynamic nation in the South Seas, and the only country in the world with a continent to itself. The vast land—nearly 3 million square miles in extent—ranges from populous coastal strips to the empty, arid plains of the outback.

9

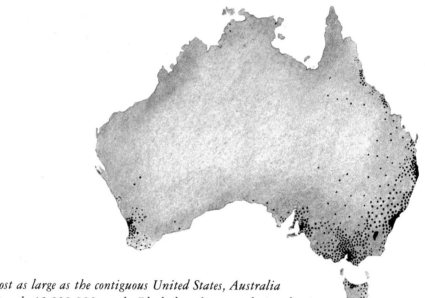

Almost as large as the contiguous United States, Australia holds only 12,000,000 people. Black dots show population density.

rounding the curve of the earth. Gliding southwest on a sea as calm as breathing, we felt winter slip astern and the Southern Hemisphere summer settle over us — the first major change we noticed. Down under the Equator, we peered into the dazzling center of the Milky Way, far richer in stars than the outer edge visible from the earth's northern half. The affairs of man, too, seemed altered, with news of the world crackling over shortwave more vicarious now, a story involving somebody else.

And the emptiness! Officers on watch in South Pacific waters sight other vessels with binoculars and radar. But passengers rarely see the distant rags of smoke by day, the tiny sparks of light at night, that sprinkle shipping lanes in more crowded parts of the world.

We did not have to know, in precise terms, that Australia holds hardly more citizens than metropolitan New York City in an area almost as large as the contiguous United States. We felt it — a sense of massive spaciousness that begins far out to sea and grows stronger still on the vast, vacant sprawl of the continent.

"Two small craft dead ahead." An officer at the wheelhouse telephone relayed the message from a lookout on the bow. Captain Wright scanned the sea, then handed me a pair of binoculars. I watched a small cabin cruiser pitch seaward over the swells, then veer south toward the area where the jet was landing near Botany Bay. The other boat, a trim yawl with *Judith Anne* painted on her stern, turned northward. Sails starched stiffly in a wind abaft, she rolled along the watery trail that His Majesty's Bark *Endeavour* blazed with the first Europeans to see this coast.

"We steer'd along shore NNE," the captain of the British ship, James Cook, wrote in his journal on May 6, 1770, "and at Noon we were ... about 2 or 3 Miles from the land and abreast of a Bay or Harbour wherein there apper'd to be safe anchorage which I call'd *Port Jackson*."

The Pacific explorer did not discover the whole Australian continent. By the time he sailed past the site of present-day Sydney, the Dutch, trading with the Spice Islands of Indonesia, had already charted the north and west coasts, half of the southern shore, and Tasmania, the present island state 150 miles off the continent's southeastern tip. But they sought gold or spice. And they found nothing at all worth trade. So the land waited, unwanted, until Captain Cook discovered the fertile east coast. He claimed most of Australia's eastern half for Britain, and settlers later extended the claim 2,489 miles wide, all the way to the Indian Ocean.

The *Mariposa* steamed across Cook's course and land ahead came clear, leaping grandly from the sea, splashed with surf and sudden bursts of sunlight. The entrance to Port Jackson — or Sydney Harbour as people usually call it today — yawned wide between flat-topped tan promontories. "Outer North Head," the captain pointed, "240 feet high . . . Outer South Head, 270 feet . . . both stratified sandstone." And, he made it a point to mention, the land we looked upon was very, very old.

Charts in the wheelhouse showed hints of continental age. Eons of the ocean's boom and whoosh had chewed most of the coastline, 12,446 miles around, relatively free of peninsulas and bays.

Terrain beyond the coast reveals some of the oldest earth emerging from the waters. On an average, Australia rises less than 1,000 feet above sea level, compared with 2,300 feet for the rest of the world's land. Time, with its erosion from rain and wind, has worn it low. And smooth — most of the continent looks almost flat. It holds hills, of course, and mountains within its 2,967,741 square miles. But even these usually show the wear of extreme age, rolling along horizons like gentle ocean waves.

"Put her on slow ahead," Captain Wright ordered. An orange and yellow pilot boat named *Goondooloo* came bounding to our side. The pilot leaped for a dangling rope ladder. In minutes he appeared in the wheelhouse to guide us to our berth.

A S EIGHT BELLS from a round brass clock rang 8 a.m., the *Mariposa* slipped between the harbor heads. Captain Cook thought this gap might hide safe anchorage. And in 1788, the governor of Australia's first settlers, mostly convicts transported from overcrowded jails in Britain, called the harbor "the finest . . . in the world, in which a thousand sail of the line may ride in the most perfect security." Now ferryboats, tugs, flakes of colored sail, naval vessels, and ocean freighters slid about on 21 square miles of saltwater harbor spreading away to our port side.

"Ten degrees left rudder," the pilot ordered. Coming around, our bow swept past red-roofed suburbs, then faraway apartment windows glinting like tiny jewels in a lance of sunlight. "Ease to five."

"Midship . . . steady now." At six or seven knots, we crept toward a cluster of white skyscrapers still several miles away.

The city around us seemed to contradict its own continent. As large as Washington or Madrid, bigger than Rome or Vienna, it crowds 2,600,000 people on the threshold of the country's brooding emptiness like a colony of visitors in an alien land. But most Australians live that way, close to each other, close to the sea. Melbourne on the southern coast holds more people than Athens or Budapest or Istanbul. Four other coastal

cities divide another couple of million people among them. By percentage, Australia has more big-city dwellers than any other country on earth, and most of them live within an hour's drive of an ocean.

"But you have to go into the bush for the real Australia," people here will tell you. Like foreigners, they are thinking of sheepdogs, cattle, and lean bronze horsemen, as well as flightless birds seven feet tall and animals that carry their young in little front pockets. Not many people live in the bush. But bush, in many forms, covers most of Australia.

In the temperate south, it takes the shape of silent, mossy forests, more winter snowcountry than Switzerland could hold, wheatlands rolling for 200 miles at a stretch and sheeplands for a thousand. Mary Ann Harrell would see much of this region, traveling from cities to vineyards to mining country.

Hector Holthouse, a journalist from the city of Brisbane and our third co-author, would write about his native state of Queensland, a land of jungle, sugar-cane fields, and tropical reefs.

WHERE HE LEFT OFF at the far-north town of Cairns, I would begin, moving inland over thirsty cattle country and a bush full of crocodiles, tropical birds, and wild buffalo herds. Out west, I'd find a deathly bush of enormous deserts and desolate rock mountains, and there I'd also find lively promise of rich new mining strikes and modern boomtowns. Then, through the wide horizons of the region called the Centre, I'd see cattlemen and tribal Aborigines living in semidesert bush a thousand miles and more from busy cities.

Our combined itinerary for the enormous country was simple, shaped like a curl. Beginning on the southern coast, at the city of Adelaide, it drew a counterclockwise circle all the way around the continent, then a straight line to the center.

The *Mariposa* glided past the costly homes of Vaucluse suburb. "Right 20 degrees," the pilot ordered and we rounded Bradley Head where Sydney's zoo hides in a eucalyptus forest. "Hard right." The foremast slipped into line with Sydney Harbour Bridge, its gray girders vaulting so high that ships at sea can sight the arch from 30 miles away.

Tugboats began to fret and toot around the bow and stern. The *Mariposa* veered hard left. It took only minutes to slip into Woolloomooloo Bay, past two aircraft carriers and five smaller ships berthed in the slender channel. At the end, seamen hurled thin rope heaving lines ashore. Dockworkers stopped their game of badminton and hauled thick rope hawsers from the ship, looping them over big steel bollards on the wharf. Capstans tugged the hawsers taut. The ship eased snug to land.

Disembarking almost in the center of Sydney, I hailed a taxi. The car crept through thick traffic on narrow downtown streets, then moved into more spacious southern suburbs toward the airport at Botany Bay. There both Mary Ann and I would begin our Australian journeys.

Racing fans crowd elbow-to-elbow at the Melbourne Cup, their nation's Kentucky Derby. Intent faces reflect diversity: One in six Australians immigrated.

Lifeblood of a dry land: Australia's major river—and one of its few dependable water sources—the Murray (opposite) courses below the Snowy Mountains, part of the Great Dividing Range that separates the fertile east coast and the harsh interior. Unreliable rivers like Queensland's Norman (above) shrink to scattered water holes during drought, and flood miles-wide after heavy rains.

The hot, red center: Salt ridges (opposite) pattern dry Lake Eyre in South Australia. "The very sight of it creates thirst in man and beast," wrote a 19th-century surveyor. Nearby, a "gibber" plain—from an Aboriginal word for stone—stretches toward eroded hills. Palms, remnants of tropical vegetation that once covered central Australia, survive in the Northern Territory's Palm Valley.

TED SPIEGEL, RAPHO GUILLUMETTE

Pasture shaded by groves of eucalypts provides graze for a mob of sheep in Western Australia's wheat belt, where an average annual rainfall of 15 inches waters grain crops. Four-fifths of the continent

receives so little rain that some huge outback sheep stations require as much as 40 acres to support a single animal. Australia supplies almost a third of the world's wool, but turns increasingly to manufacturing.

2

On the Boomerang Coast, Home to Most Australians

MARY ANN HARRELL

THE WORLD'S GREATEST BOOMERANG — Australia's Boomerang Coast — holds a sweep of land as distinctive and unforgettable as an Aborigine's throwing stick dark against the sun. The name echoes a tribal word; the shape evokes an archaic design. But in other respects this region owes its character to the 180 years since the first Englishmen came.

For weeks I traveled along this graceful curve of the continent. I found its people hospitable, yet reserved; optimistic, yet aware of the have-not world from which prosperity sets them apart. For today life runs pleasantly here, with strenuous sports and easy-going manners, Coonawarra clarets and spaghetti on toast, skyscrapers clear-cut as ice and suburbs as expansive as spilled paint.

This region stretches for 1,700 miles around the southeastern edge of Australia. It holds less than one-tenth of the nation's land — and eight out of every ten people. The boomerang's shorter arm begins at Port Pirie, on Spencer Gulf, and extends beyond Adelaide to Melbourne. Its longer arm reaches northeast, tapering out above Brisbane. Beyond this arc — inland and along the coasts — the uncrowded distances begin.

Australia measures rainfall by the point, 1/100 of an inch; concentrates her people; and spreads her prosperity with amazing evenness for a life of contentment. I noticed all this quickly in Adelaide, capital of South Australia. "We're the driest state in the driest continent" — I heard this

Watching wine's mysterious alchemy, a third-generation vintner studies a sample of dry red aging in an oak cask. Outside the cool, dark cellar, the sun warms South Australia's Barossa Valley, where grapes in heavy clusters yield a fourth of the country's annual production of 45 million gallons of wine.

TED SPIEGEL, RAPHO GUILLUMETTE

21

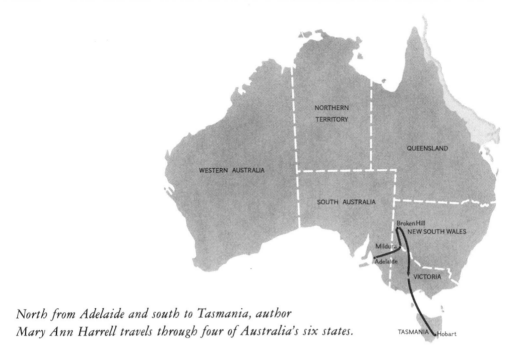

North from Adelaide and south to Tasmania, author
Mary Ann Harrell travels through four of Australia's six states.

repeatedly. Horizonsful of arid space lie empty, while greater Adelaide has almost two-thirds of the state's entire population. Within the city's area of 170 square miles live 726,930 people.

I arrived in the midst of preparations for Adelaide's fifth Festival of Arts—"a true popular celebration," its administrator Max Lamshed told me, "not a party for stiff shirts and stilted minds. For 1968 we're turning a restaurant in the South Parklands into a sort of Bavarian beer garden. Every night we'll have free entertainment, in a Continental atmosphere. We're acquiring a sophistication that we've never had before."

For the first time, the Festival authorities had commissioned a play, Patricia Hooker's comedy *The Lotos Eaters*—a satire on labor-management relations and Australian attitudes toward work or leisure.

I watched the city dress up her finest avenues for a fortnight of fun, with flags, bunting, and strings of colored lights. On a bright Saturday afternoon I walked down to Elder Park, joining parents and grandparents to lounge on the grass while junior bandsmen in red tunics gallantly attacked "The Caisson Song." Soloists ran through "Tea for Two" and "Moonlight Bay." Junior and Senior Twirlettes spun their shining batons; girls from the Adelaide College of Dancing spun their pirouettes.

In the midst of the metropolitan area, Saturday sports find a perfect setting, with tennis courts and football fields, two 18-hole golf courses, bowling greens, croquet grounds, and a racecourse scattered among 1,700 acres of parkland. One grassy loop rings North Adelaide; another surrounds the business district.

Adelaide owes its unrivaled design to a stalwart Englishman, Col. William Light, who reached Australia at the age of 50. He had fought in some 40 battles against Napoleon's armies; married a beautiful, pipe-smoking heiress who deserted him; and recruited English seamen for the unsuccessful dream navy of the pasha of Egypt. Then he accepted the post of surveyor-general for South Australia, a dream colony that succeeded.

Leading an advance party, Light decided to set the capital of the colony near the Gulf of St. Vincent, "on a beautiful and gently rising ground." In January, 1837, he was "devising in my own mind the best method of laying out the town." He went on to survey 150,000 acres of bush before he died exhausted, aged 53. In his honor, the city fathers of 1858 voted £10 annually "for Colonial wine and biscuit that the citizens may drink to the memory of Colonel Light." At the Town Hall, officials explained the ceremony for me. Aldermen and Councillors take their places, and the Clerk enters in white wig and dark robe. A macebearer precedes the Right Honourable the Lord Mayor, who offers the toast to Colonel Light. Then all the dignitaries drink it in silence. "We serve Australian sherry," the Clerk's assistant told me, "but instead of biscuit we have fruitcake today."

SUCH MOMENTS OF RITUAL help account for Adelaide's reputation for being more English than England used to be. From early days the town has taken pride in her sense of decorum. Her leading citizens rode out in top hats and frock coats to escort explorer Edward John Eyre when he began an expedition northward into wilderness in June, 1840.

Yet for all these echoes of England, Adelaide's climate seems triumphantly Mediterranean. And often I compared Australia's south with my own, back in the Carolinas. I felt at home in the easy pace of things, the sociable greetings that friends exchange on downtown streets, the talk of kinship — grandfathers, in-laws, and cousins. "Here everyone knows everyone else," my new acquaintances assured me; "that's why we can put on the Festival. Everybody cooperates, you see."

Beyond the interest in genealogy, I found that a concern for progress marks this "new south" nowadays. I discussed these common goals with P. W. Whicker, of the South Australian Housing Trust, as we drove out from Adelaide toward its new satellite city, Elizabeth. "South Australia has become very progressive since World War II," he said. "Prior to that it was a rural state. By 1948 it was fast becoming industrialized, and attracting a high percentage of all migrants to Australia. We could foresee a housing shortage, and the Trust started planning Elizabeth as a self-sufficient town, not just another suburb."

We jolted up an unpaved track to a ridge overlooking miles of plain. Mr. Whicker pointed out the industrial sites, where General Motors-Holden's Pty. Ltd. employs 5,250 people, where other firms manufacture sewing machines, forklift trucks, storage batteries, machine tools, gases, sports clothes, fireworks.

"Just 12 years ago all that was pasture, or fields planted in wheat and barley and oats," Mr. Whicker told me. "Now more than 46,000 people live there. We're adding a thousand houses a year, some 45 percent for rental. A man with a large family, making about $40 [$44.80 U. S.] a week, can rent a home with three bedrooms for $8 to $11 a week.*

"About 50 percent of the people here come from the United Kingdom and Europe," Mr. Whicker explained. "The federal government will help

*Unless otherwise indicated, all monetary references in this book are expressed in Australian dollars.

pay their passage, and the Trust has a London office that handles thousands of immigration inquiries. We meet these people before they leave, and assist them before and after they arrive. It's a big change, from narrow dark streets in Birmingham and London to all this."

By 1980, the planners expect, a single linear city of one million will extend along the coast north and south of the capital and its port. Percy F. Pollnitz of the South Australian Government Tourist Bureau sketched its prospect as we stood at Windy Point in the Mount Lofty Ranges, a chain of rolling hills east of Adelaide. Suburbs ran on below, dimmed by light haze.

"We're trying now to provide parks for the future," he said as we drove on through the hills. We saw Sunday games and picnics in the bush — woods, to me — at Belair National Park. And I cuddled my first koala, a plaintive, drowsy bundle of fur named Lindy, in the new Native Fauna Reserve of Cleland National Park. There John Neale, the assistant curator, joined us. "We only opened in April, 1967," Mr. Neale reported, "and already we're averaging almost 3,000 visitors a week. It seems this was something the public wanted."

One thing people certainly want is good wine. Australia's home market for table wine quadrupled between 1955 and 1967 — to almost six million imperial gallons. Including sherry and dessert wines, Australians are drinking about seventeen million gallons a year.

Northeast of Adelaide and Elizabeth sprawls the rolling open country of the Barossa Valley, where descendants of Lutheran refugees from Germany have developed the art of wine-making for four generations. "They still speak German at home," remarked Reye Wright, a tanned, skin-diving connoisseur from Adelaide who escorted me through the country. "They bake fine apfelstrudel, and bring out 19th-century schnapps for funerals or christenings."

HILLS SLUMP into plain farther northeast. Sheep nibble pastures pale gold in early sun. I followed the Sturt Highway, named for the explorer who fought his way northward after Eyre turned back from glittering salt pans and mountains he named Deception and Hopeless.

Charles Sturt took his party up the Murray and the Darling Rivers in 1844, noticing veins of metal near present-day Broken Hill. He struggled 800 miles before he reached the area near the continent's heart where men expected to find a great inland sea. Instead of sea, he found drought; heat that splintered pencils; subfreezing cold in June. But he won all his races with drying waterholes to reach Adelaide again in January, 1846.

Billboards disappear quickly from his route. Stretches of bare yellow-gray soil widen between the stumpy or spindly gum trees. Eventually the road crosses the Murray, lavishly blue. For the first time in my life, I wanted to cheer for a river. Occasional glimpses of the stream break vacant miles of rippling, reddish sand. A sign hails the border of the State of Victoria; then dustdevils provide elusive landmarks. A brick-colored soil holds clumps of blue-gray-green saltbush.

I never expected irrigation to be exhilarating, but I remember the area around the town of Mildura as a festival of water. In concrete channels

*Closing in for the kill, a
Tasmanian wolf bounds after
a brush-tailed wallaby. Although
the last of the wolflike marsupials
in captivity died in Hobart in 1935, some
may still roam Tasmania's high country.
The creature's scientific name,* Thylacinus
cynocephalus, *means "the pouched dog with a wolf head."*

water brims forward, generous as a symphony. T-shaped overhead sprinklers spin with the poise of ballerinas. Citrus trees hold their dense green in ordered ranks among vineyards.

Mildurans ask proudly, "Have you seen our new arts center?" I admired its crisp contemporary lines; but I spent more time in the Victorian house that adjoins it, a museum honoring W. B. Chaffey, Canadian-born hero of irrigation in California and in the Murray Valley. With his brother George, he fought through the 1890's—against rabbits, droughts, floods, labor troubles, grasshoppers, and bank panics—to establish the pumps and pipes and organization that turn the desolate country into gold. For, as everyone says, "This land will grow *anything* — if you can get water onto it."

"We marketed two and a half million bushels in 1966," said Kevin R. Pickering of the Sunraysia District Citrus Cooperative Society, Ltd. "We expect five million by 1975. Mostly Valencia oranges, but also navels, mandarins, grapefruits, lemons, and Sevilles for marmalade. We have some frost trouble, but less than Florida's. In a good year, like 1967, we get about $7,000,000."

Most of the grape harvest goes for raisins. Peter Lindsay and his father Fred explained sun-drying for me as they worked at it on their 40-acre holding. They dip the grapes into a carbonate-of-potash and emulsified-oil solution, then spread them on nine-tier racks to shrivel in the sun.

Salt threatens both vines and orchards when the river runs low. L. G. Cameron, of the Australian Dried Fruits Association, told me: "These soils hold salt from an ancient inland sea. We've had to live with that. But when the percentage of salt in the river rises, as it does when the volume of water falls, we're very much worried. We're trying to apply the best new techniques of irrigation that agricultural scientists can teach us. And we want to ensure that the Murray-Darling waters are preserved—in quantity and quality, unpolluted."

Once the region depended on these waters for transportation. But railroads doomed the old sidewheelers. Capt. W. E. Collins, who's building a home ashore to retire to, took me to meet his sister, Capt. Pearl Hogg—"she and her husband both hold engineer's and master's tickets"—and their mother, Mrs. William C. Collins, who never held either license but could handle either job.

With tales of the 29 steamers the family has owned, these three experts carried me from one wharf and one year to another, along streams more capricious than Mark Twain's Mississippi. They unrolled oldtime charts, calico strips with cryptic serpents outlined in India ink, place names every few feet, red dots for sandbars. Captain Bill confirmed my suspicion—a skipper who didn't know the river already could never read these charts.

As Captain Pearl put it, you read the river: "You learn to know what's beneath you, a snag or a rock, by the ripples, the shape of the water, all the different disturbances. There's always something—a tree maybe—to let you know where you are." "And," Captain Bill added: "You had to *know* it, all. It was a question of men's lives."

LIFE HAS CHANGED DRAMATICALLY at Broken Hill, 170 miles north in New South Wales. Here, in the Barrier Ranges, veins of treasure reached up to the sunlight: the famous "line of lode," as the town proudly calls its rich deposit of lead, zinc, and silver.

"Two world wars and a depression and two big strikes, I've seen the good with the bad here," remarked city librarian Allan Coulls, bringing out relics of the "Barrier rush" that started in 1883. He displayed iron shoes for bullocks of pre-railroad years, a letter dated February 2, 1888: "... here as in America there is but little starch in society.... the rough element strongly predominates." He brought out a rare pay docket, dated April 28, 1897: After deductions for stores and explosives, a party of nine men had earned a penny apiece per shift.

Today the miners of Broken Hill claim high pay and equally high living standards. "After the long strike in 1919-1920, all the unions here got together and formed the Barrier Industrial Council," explained J. P. Keenan, a youthful veteran of 30 years underground and senior vice-president of the B.I.C.

"Elsewhere in Australia," he continued, "most industrial disputes go before government arbitrators. Not here. The B.I.C. officers sit down with management every three years and review everything. When we disagree, we really thrash it out. Once we make an agreement, it's the Bible. We haven't had any long strikes for many years.

"It's not all beer and skittles here. There's poverty, too. We strive to improve things for everybody. We've got to look to the future, for our sons and daughters. Automation ... it's not creeping in, it's flying in."

At the Zinc Corporation, Ltd., general manager J. L. Liebelt gave me his view of Broken Hill as a place to live and work in. He discussed rising costs, economic extraction of low-grade ore, recent advances in metallurgy, and concluded: "I've visited most large mining fields in the world, and I've not yet seen another I'd prefer."

At the fringe of civilization, Broken Hill relays its messages to lonely sheep stations by radio. Its Royal Flying Doctor base copes with medical problems for an area the size of seven Englands, and lends its transmitters to the School of the Air for two classroom sessions a day. Currently, these include about 100 children in three states. One Thursday morning I heard Miss Marie Gordon and Miss Joyce Percival lead the songs and news talks, discuss definitions of a sentence, and plan for a play on Friday. Their second graders spoke up politely by name and call sign. In "The Gingerbread Boy," Cheryl would play the old tin kettle and Stephen—some 120 miles distant—would play the red-and-white cow.

Isolation remains, even in town. As one mine employee told me, laughing: "Australia's where Broken Hill people go on holidays."

And on holidays, Australia's island state of Tasmania draws visitors from all the rest of the nation—and the world—with mountain parks, open green valleys that could almost be in Devon, late-Georgian homes, and shiny motels of a new prosperity. If I could choose an ideal vacation there, I would hike through the back country with a zoological expedition, one that would find a living thylacine—Tasmania's wolflike marsupial. Perhaps in the little-known ranges it still stalks small wallabies, but quite possibly the last survivor died in the wilds 20 years ago.

Yet the lowlands tell much of the state's story, as Jim and Mary Warner quickly proved to me. Longtime friends of NATIONAL GEOGRAPHIC editor Howell Walker, they gave me lunch and lessons at Valleyfield, their home near the Derwent River. "We think this is the oldest continuously inhabited house in the state," Mary said. "It was licensed as a coach road pub, the King's Head Inn, in 1822."

Jim hurried off to preparations for the hops harvest and Mary led me through its setting. We inspected the spindly vines, picking a cluster of the green cones that give beer its flavor. In a three-story shed we walked past 80 feet of burly new machinery fixed in concrete. "This monster whips the vines along among wires to strip leaves and twigs from the cones," she pointed out.

At the orchard Jim showed me his new packing equipment for apples, Tasmania's other traditional crop. "Once the Northern Hemisphere depended on us for its out-of-season pome fruit," he said. "Now European growers can keep apples in gas storage and sell them with lower shipping costs. We need new markets. There're many people in India who would buy our apples, but they're scattered all over the place; how do you reach them? For the past five years we've been sending our big apples to Hong Kong; street vendors quarter them and sell them by the slice."

I saw the country in a dry year. Blackened eucalypts traced the sweep of a disastrous bushfire in 1967, but green sprigs showed regeneration at work. Fields normally green lay dull gold.

With ample rainfall the rule, and snow on the highlands in winter, Tasmania relies on hydroelectric power for her growing towns and industries. At the newest installation, water from the Savage River carries finely ground iron ore from inland mines through a pipeline 53 miles long to Port Latta. Here a pelletizing plant prepares the ore for shipment: 45 million tons in the next 20 years, by current contracts. A conveyor system runs it out more than a mile offshore for bulk loading on freighters Japan-bound via Bass Strait.

Those waters, often stormy, kept Tasmania remote from "the other side" — Melbourne, Darwin, all those places. Yet Hobart, with her superb harbor, rivaled Sydney by 1820 and surpassed her as a whaling port in the 1840's. "Many years ago," a lady assured me with proper civic pride, "Hobart was the roughest city in the world. Now you hear, 'Sydney for holidays, Melbourne to shop, Hobart to retire in.' " A third of the island's 380,000 people live in greater Hobart, but a country-town flavor remains.

ABOVE THE WATERFRONT stands the state Parliament House. Clerk-Assistant Bruce Murphy escorted me through the green-carpeted sanctum of the House of Assembly and the crimson-decked hall of the Legislative Council. Here, on January 25, 1886, delegates held the first session of the Federal Council of Australasia, forerunner of the present Commonwealth born January 1, 1901. And in the old vaults below, Bruce pointed out a grim token of sovereignty. "See the Broad Arrow on those bricks? It means 'government property.' They're the work of convicts."

For the island, then called Van Diemen's Land, entered history in 1803 as part of the world's largest prison. A little museum at Port Arthur displays faded lists in clerkly handwriting: William Barlow, 14, potter; for stealing cheese, seven years. James Lynch, 9; for stealing three boxes of toys, seven years. After 1835 such youngsters could learn a trade in a settlement reserved for them. The penitentiary at Port Arthur held hard cases in solitary confinement.

"A terribly gruesome history, this place," say the guides. They keep up a patter of time-tested jokes, "to keep you from crying," as they shepherd their charges through the somber ruins. "Now, this model prison replaced flogging with solitude; here they tormented men's *minds*. You'd never see another prisoner. They'd put a bag over your head to take you to the chapel. . . ." Among its ivy-loosened tawny stones, I could see the shadowy hooded figures . . . and, on the rear wall, a lighthearted inscription that I, for one, would not erase: "DIANNE LOVES DAVID 1967."

Another cheerful comment came from Dr. R. A. Lewis of Hobart. He belongs to the state's National Trust, a voluntary organization to preserve historic buildings. From him I learned that today many Tasmanians see a fresh value and beauty in homes their forebears built in early colonial days. He emphasized the pride young people take in their heritage, concluding happily: "The future is in good hands."

Ballet students perform basic exercises at the Arts Centre in Mildura, hub of a major irrigation project in Victoria. The Centre also houses a museum and theater.

Adelaide, capital and commercial center of South Australia, rises amid playing fields and parklands that stretch in green loops through the city. For Saturday sports residents flock to cricket or football

fields, tennis courts, golf links, and bowling greens. Balancing culture with the outdoor life, Adelaide sponsors fêtes of music, drama, and art. Most famous: the Festival of Arts, staged every other March.

31

Lunch-hour athletics provide an energetic interlude for workers at the General Motors-Holden's automobile plant at Elizabeth, a planned industrial city of 46,000 outside Adelaide. Sandwich in hand, a bowler (left) spins a ball down the "green," a carpet unfurled daily for a game of bowls in the engineering department. The scorekeeper (opposite below) holds calipers, ready to determine a close roll. A mechanic sights a dart (above), and a competitor (below left) takes a turn. A soccer game absorbs limber-limbed employees near a row of partially assembled Holdens outside the company's paint shop. Spectators below lunch from Gladstone bags.

TED SPIEGEL, RAPHO GUILLUMETTE

Once an arid waste, the Murray River valley blooms here with vineyards, citrus groves, and orchards watered by a vast network of channels and pipelines. Since the late 19th century, irrigation has wrested more than 2.7 million acres from the grip of a hostile land.

TED SPIEGEL, RAPHO GUILLUMETTE

Outpost of industry, the town of Broken Hill draws wealth from a gigantic silver-lead-zinc lode in western New South Wales, annually producing 2.5 million tons of ore. A diesel scoop tram driven by King Rapley (below) loads rock shattered by blasting. Lunching 3,000 feet down, miners sit in year-round ventilated comfort near 70° F. On weekends men like Rapley and Don Prenzel—with cup—enjoy a fringe benefit (pages 38-39). Above ground, twilight burnishes Argent Street, business center for 30,000 residents. At the Broken Hill branch of Australia's School of the Air, a teacher discusses a geography lesson with pupils living on remote homesteads.

Miners take to boats at Menindee Lake, a man-made oasis near the Darling River, 60 miles southeast of Broken Hill. Below, scoop-tram driver King Rapley towels vigorously after a water-ski run; at right, Don Prenzel rounds a marker buoy during a race. On shore, a young teacher takes time from her charges, and in the shallows children forget their classes. The strains of "Waltzing Matilda" end a picnic (above).

TED SPIEGEL, RAPHO GUILLUMETTE

Glow of dawn on the Derwent River estuary mutes the lights of Hobart, capital of Tasmania and shipping center
40 *for the island state's huge apple crop. Above, on the Tasman Peninsula, stand the ruins of old Port Arthur, once*

*e site of a British penal col-
y, now a haunt for campers.*

*Sailmaker in a waterfront loft shapes Dacron for a pleasure yacht.
Earlier Hobart craftsmen made sails for whalers and clipper ships.* 41

Breakfast of eggs, chops, sausages, toast, and tea prepares harvest hands for a day in the fields in Tasmania's fertile northwest. Hungry gulls eat later, when
a tractor-drawn rake stirs up insects in a patch
of green peas. Nearby, a mobile viner picks and
shells pods. A logger's ax cuts cleanly in a standing-
block chopping contest at Burnie, northern Tasmania's major deepwater port and an export center
42   for paper, timber, farm produce, and minerals.

3

Melbourne, Canberra, and Men Who Capture Rivers

MARY ANN HARRELL

"GRAY? You see hardly any gray in Australian cities." Robin Boyd, distinguished as architect and writer, was guiding me through Melbourne on a Friday afternoon. We had just set out from the central area, where glossy new office blocks challenge church spires above stolid banks and shops. Crisply and wittily, he was introducing me to the city's past and to much of the continent's present.

"You see bright colors and clear pastels: hot, flat, sharp pink and yellow and sky blue; unmuted colors. Red roofs out in the suburbs, usually." Creeping through inchworm traffic, we compared notes on Melbourne —714 square miles of urban sprawl from the busy harbor, Port Phillip, to low mountain ranges on the horizon.

Suddenly Mr. Boyd called my attention to new government buildings: "You'll notice that they are more subdued." As capital of the State of Victoria, Melbourne builds more and more of these, but the styles of Queen Victoria's reign still mark the city with sober structures in dark bluestone. "Luckily," my host remarked, "we built most of them early enough to escape the worst 19th-century wedding cake."

Founded in 1835 by free settlers from Tasmania, Melbourne spread with astonishing speed along the Yarra. "It's a fairly miserable little river, but we love it," Mr. Boyd commented when we crossed it. Gold spurred things on after 1851. Men rushed inland to the diggings at Bendigo and

Christmas shoppers and homebound commuters scramble in Melbourne, financial capital of Australia. Bourke Street, washed by the warm rain of summer in the Southern Hemisphere, leads to colonnaded Parliament House, seat of government for the State of Victoria. Beyond soar the spires of St. Patrick's Cathedral.

From Melbourne, the author traces the Snowy Mountains Hydro-electric Scheme, then visits Canberra, the nation's capital.

Ballarat; immigrants swarmed in by the shipload; canvas suburbs sprang up. Before long, brick replaced tents. Now many old houses have come down in slum-clearance schemes. "You might not recognize the slums as such," he said, "but the children have nowhere to play except the street. Now the state government is building high-rise units in prefabricated concrete and subsidizing rents as low as $2 a week for a single elderly person."

In 1960, my guide had published *The Australian Ugliness,* a study of gaudy billboards, clashing styles of architecture, fidgety and lavish decoration. I asked if he had noticed a change since then. "Yes," he replied with a smile. "Now one can criticize without being called un-Australian."

Nevertheless, I wouldn't want to lead a campaign against horse racing in Australia. I would certainly be called a "wowser," Australian for "killjoy." Besides, I enjoyed myself immensely on the first day of the autumn meeting at the Caulfield course. The heat reached 107° F., and an elderly man told me, "Only the greedy'd come today." A small crowd of 14,000 did. In the Members' Ladies' stand, women in flowered hats and white gloves checked the odds and cheered decorously. In the public stands, tanned men in sports shirts yelled the favorite in the fifth race to a three-way photo finish—"Come on, Magic! *Come on, Jim!"* —and gave the winning jockey a drawled-out deep chorus, "Good-on-yer, Jim!"

Australians keep their wildest cheers for the underdog, and the underdog who shows outstanding courage against odds may win the supreme compliment, "as game as Ned Kelly." Last and greatest of the bushrangers, the "bad men" of Australia's "Wild East," Ned Kelly first tangled with the law in 1869, at the age of 14. Soon he took to the hills with his brother Dan and two other young outlaws to lead the police a long and often ludicrous chase. He coolly collected funds from unlucky banks, and won the whole-hearted sympathy of many who disliked the powers that be— street-corner boys in Melbourne, Irish immigrants with no love for the Crown, small farmers at odds with great landholders.

Finally, in 1880, the police had the Kelly gang bailed up—cornered—at the minute town of Glenrowan for a 12-hour siege. In daybreak fog Ned stalked out wearing homemade armor forged from stolen plough-shares—to go down with a collection of bullet wounds, stand trial undaunted in Melbourne, and die on the gallows as a convicted murderer, widely mourned. Today the people who keep his name alive will support overmatched foreign athletes against the home team, if the outsiders make Ned Kelly's kind of courageous stand.

HAD A CHANCE to inquire about Australian industry, new and old, since Melbourne serves as financial center for the country. I visited the home office of the biggest firm of all, and Derek Sawer explained why the Broken Hill Proprietary Company Ltd. is working almost every mineral site except its namesake town. "We had only the center portion of that lode, and we mined it out. We left there in 1939." Today B.H.P. quarries iron ore in the west and manganese at Groote Eylandt in the north, mines coal not far from Sydney on the eastern coast, makes more and more steel, builds ships at Whyalla in South Australia.

In a 50-50 partnership with Standard Oil, B.H.P. has struck it lucky. Their first offshore well in Bass Strait tapped a great reservoir of natural gas; pipelines now under construction will supply gas to Melbourne. And in March, 1968, the partners almost doubled their first estimates on oil from the Bass Strait fields. They predicted 240,000 barrels a day by late 1970, nearly half the country's total requirement.

"For the first time, it appears that Australia might be self-sufficient in oil," said Noel Buckley of Standard Oil. "A few years ago, the experts didn't expect this. Now we count on more discoveries, and the offshore area looks like the most promising."

But the oldest source of the nation's wealth, wool, faces the most troubled future. At the headquarters of the Australian Wool Board, key organization of the industry, J. T. O'Keefe of the senior staff summed up the prospect. "Today wool provides less than eight percent of the world's fiber. Possibly by the year 2000 this will sink to less than four percent because of increased use of synthetic materials.

"It's still true that 'Australia rides on the sheep's back,' although you don't hear the old saying so often. We lead the world in wool production by a wide margin, and wool earns almost a third of our total export income—about $870 million for 1966-67. Japan's our best customer now, taking 32 percent of the clip. More and more, our wool growers visit the markets: Milano, New York, London, Tokyo. And today," he added, "we have science on our side."

For all the sophistication of agricultural research, drought can still drive graziers into debt or even off their land. Months without adequate rain had dragged over Victoria and New South Wales before my visit. Greater Melbourne's 2,270,000 citizens watched their reserves of water slip lower: enough for 89 days, 88, 87.... The states banned all outdoor burning, but a bushfire claimed 54 suburban homes in the Dandenong Ranges, 20 miles from the city.

Inland from Melbourne, miles of grazing country lay heartbreak brown, burned by the sun. Not until April was the drought finally broken. Looking down from a speeding plane, I remembered a friend's summary: "We've got the world's biggest rivers. They just don't have any water in them." These channels run inland into desert. In past years even the Murray almost ran dry, or ran wild in flood, stranding its steamboats in shrinking pools or permitting them to cruise across the plains. And only the Murray system offers a reasonably reliable supply west of the Great Dividing Range. As an Australian geologist told me, "God put our mountains too near the east coast." For centuries most of the water they collected spilled idly into the Tasman Sea.

Now SMA, the Snowy Mountains Hydro-electric Authority, turns water westward for farms and sends electricity eastward for cities. A deceptively simple matter: Pull together small mountain streams, store the water behind dams, pour it through tunnels to generate power, send

Side-wheel steamer pauses between flooded gum trees to unload provisions at a homestead on the rain-swollen Murray River. Skilled pilots avoided shoals, rocks, and other hazards by reading the river's swirls and ripples. Once a principal means of transport, the boats eventually lost their trade to trains, trucks, and planes, making their last cargo runs in the 1950's.

RICHARD SCHLECHT

it down the Murray and Murrumbidgee valleys for irrigation — as needed. Begun in 1949 and now about three-fourths completed, the Snowy Scheme is one of the engineering wonders of the world. It embraces more than 2,500 square miles of rough terrain, administered from Cooma in southeastern New South Wales.

At Cooma I met Charles Stanford of SMA, and we climbed into a small helicopter to trace the waters through the highest country in Australia, snow-covered half the year.

"See those empty creeks? Old-timers said they would never dry up in any drought," Charley called above the noise. Then we reached man-made Lake Eucumbene, heart of the system, pale blue below barren ribbons of shore. "It's unusually low from three years' light runoff. The irrigation areas are using more water." I remembered the lavish acres at Mildura. "This is the year water was needed, and we've got it." He pointed north. "Over there's the tunnel for the Tumut Development, the one that supplies the Murrumbidgee." We swung above drowned trees and on to the ponderous dam, almost half a mile thick at the base.

My respect for the mountains and the engineers who mastered them grew stronger with each mile as Charley directed us above a 14-mile tunnel to Tumut Pond Reservoir. Through a steep-walled gorge we reached Happy Jacks Dam. "That's where we send the Tumut River down if we want to," Charley explained. The gorge runs 2,000 feet deep. "It's a huge gutter, like your Grand Canyon," he remarked.

Later, easing down into afternoon heat, we took a car to the surface power station called Murray 1. Inside, ten turbogenerators spin out 95,000 kilowatts each at a steady 50-cycle hum. Before starting homeward we circled the site of Murray 2, where hardworking water finds a sunlit course westward at last.

Men from the Snowy have moved on to southeast Asia — by orders from Canberra, of course. In Australia's federal capital, I found clear proof of the Commonwealth's concern for the Near North, the lands that Britons and Americans have called the Far East. At the Department of External Affairs, Assistant Secretary L. W. Engledow gave me examples of aid for the nation's neighbors. "We thought the Snowy teams too valuable to disband. They're free-wheeling types who get things done. They're helping Thai engineers build roads in mountainous country near the Burma border. They designed Cambodia's big dam at Prek Thnot, and they're studying other sites on the Mekong River."

From the Prime Minister, the Rt. Hon. John Grey Gorton, I heard a family example of this concern with Asia. His American-born wife Bettina recently took her bachelor's degree in Oriental studies at the Australian National University. "She broadcasts to Indonesia on women's programs," he said, "but since I took this office she has had to stop her work on a Malayan-English dictionary."

Australia's federal system mixes British and American elements. Its Parliament comprises the Crown, represented by a Governor-General; a Senate, with ten members from each state; and a House of Representatives, with seats allotted on a basis of population. Every Prime Minister before

Mr. Gorton held a seat in the House, where national policies must win approval. But after the death of Mr. Harold Holt in 1967, the Liberal Party broke tradition to choose Senator Gorton to lead the Government. He resigned from the upper chamber to campaign for a Representative's seat; and so I met the only Prime Minister to date without a seat in Parliament.

"As in England," he said, "the Prime Minister and his Cabinet are responsible to the Parliament. The Government usually resigns if it loses a vote of confidence in the House. Therefore we don't have anything like the U. S. Congressional committee inquiries into executive affairs." Soon he carried Mr. Holt's district in a by-election to fill the vacancy. In March he entered the House, reaching across its center table to shake hands with the Leader of the Opposition, Representative Gough Whitlam.

Australians of every party talk of the need for a larger population. A senior official at the Department of Immigration offered me his opinion: "We hope to increase the population through net immigration by about one percent annually. That's becoming more difficult as European prosperity rises and Australia becomes more industrialized. We want skilled workers; we need to recognize professional qualifications from countries besides Britain. We haven't spoken of a 'White Australia Policy' for years." This policy has limited immigration to persons of European stock. "We'll accept individual non-Europeans who offer the skills and knowledge we need, who will fit into our society. We do want to keep Australia homogeneous and stable. And we expect to reach 13 million by 1973."

Canberra's own population has doubled since 1960. In 1968 it approached 110,000; its commissioners expect 250,000 in the 1980's, a rate to make up for time lost since the dedication in 1913. Commonwealth leaders established a purely national city, like America's Founding Fathers who chose a center on the Potomac to appease state rivalries. Plans called for federal buildings grouped on one side of an artificial lake, with a civic center on the other. Like Washington, Canberra grew slowly at first; war and depression held it back. "When you first get there," a friend warned me, "you think, 'where's the town?'" It hides behind avenues of trees, behind wooded hills that divide suburbs from officialdom.

LAKE BURLEY GRIFFIN gives the city a vivid center, but during my visit, water rationing stinted the carefully tended gardens, and every conversation turned to the subject of drought. I asked Sir Mark Oliphant, the distinguished physicist, about a national topic, the prospect of using atomic energy to distill fresh water from the sea.

"Until our population reaches 30 million," he replied, "natural waters may suffice if properly conserved. Our cities must have much bigger storage systems, and long-term planning on water. Strange as it may sound, we've never had a Commonwealth policy for water supply. Now we *must* develop one. The future of the country depends very critically on finding alternatives to nature in areas of no rain. In the end, desalination will come into its own, but right now the technology changes so fast that by the time you build a nuclear reactor it's obsolete. Also, of course, agricultural scientists are developing strains of plants that will

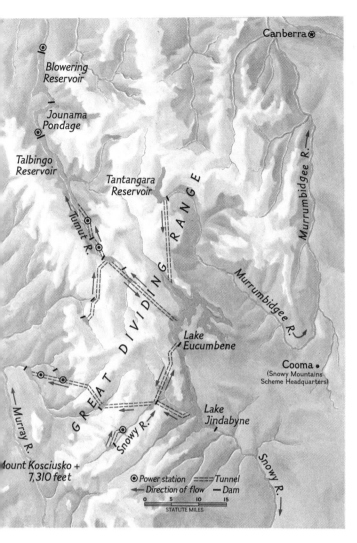

mature more quickly with a higher yield, and therefore use less water."

Wheat, corn, rice and a host of other valuable plants meet a variety of climates right in Canberra. They grow under controlled conditions in a complex called a phytotron, managed by CSIRO — the Commonwealth Scientific and Industrial Research Organisation. I shrugged myself into a white lab coat and sterile sandals to visit its greenhouse and its artificially lighted cabinets. In a refreshing, moist fragrance, Dr. Lloyd Evans explained the phytotron's role. "In the field, climate's a package deal. Here we can take a climate apart and look at individual, specific effects — temperature, humidity, day length, light intensity, wind."

Australian agriculture depends almost entirely on plants that evolved on other continents with more rain and less heat. Phytotron studies can screen existing varieties best suited to specific localities, and speed up the development of new hybrids.

Everywhere you turn in Australia, you find CSIRO. Its branch laboratories and field stations flourish in Sydney and Kojonup, Hobart and Jimboomba, Cronulla and Perth. Its staffs investigate animal genetics, fisheries, coal, mathematical statistics. With specialists from the wool industry, they study everything from sheep parasites to permanent pleating. They collaborate with university colleagues in radio astronomy, in which Australia, the United States, and the United Kingdom lead the world.

I had never seen the southern heavens before, and grudged every trace of haze or city light that dimmed the strange constellations. Only ten miles from Canberra, the Australian National University maintains an observatory among the pines on Mount Stromlo; and there, one evening, Dr. Olin Eggan made these new patterns clear.

"For years," he said, "northern countries had all the big telescopes and southern skies went neglected. But God must have loved the south – He put the good things down here. We have the closest galaxy, the Magellanic Clouds; the best examples of quasars; the brightest globular clusters – spherical clusters of stars. Astrophysics will develop much faster by access to these.

"Now we're getting a new telescope for our field station at Siding Spring – a 150-inch mirror to be ready in about five years. This will be the largest in the Southern Hemisphere, and second only to the 200-inch mirror at Palomar, in California. In the States they used to say, 'Go west, young man!' Today, for the astronomer, the word is, 'Go south!' "

ONE SHRINE I wanted to visit alone: The Australian War Memorial. Aloof on its grounds at the heart of the city, it honors all men and women who served and died in the armed forces of their country. After the full sunlight of the courtyard, the galleries seem narrow with their profusion of weapons, uniforms, paintings of battles and commanders.

Before the diorama of Gallipoli, I heard someone say: "Here we became a nation." In World War I, Anzac, code word for the Australian and New Zealand Army Corps, gave a name for a legend of sardonic courage. On the cut-up ridges above the Dardanelles, in 1915, outnumbered Anzac troops held their ground against the Turks – and attacked – until their high command ordered the survivors away.

I went on to the panels from France. One displayed the rough sign for an emergency aid station: a red cross and the words "Walking Wounded." Two boys scampered past, chattering plans for the afternoon. A white-haired attendant checked them: " 'ere, we don't want too much of that."

Silence fills the Hall of Memory. In the deep blue of stained glass stand figures in uniform, men and women, figures of Resource, Devotion, Chivalry, Curiosity, Comradeship. The dome overhead glows with mosaic in tones of the sun. At the heart of the Memorial stands a great bronze statue, the fighting man of the world wars, a hero of defiance against odds. Bronze netting drapes the marble base. Some visitors who know a Canberra custom strike this netting sharply with a fist. The bronze resounds like a bell truly cast. Its voice pervades the dome, fading slowly, an echo of thunder or cannonade among the horizon's hills.

Decked with baubles, Melbourne's Royal Arcade attracts lunch-hour buyers and browsers. Such shop-lined passageways enhance other Australian cities.

TED SPIEGEL, RAPHO GUILLUMETTE

Magnificent stained-glass ceiling 200 feet long illumines the lofty reception hall of the new National Gallery of Victoria, heart of Melbourne's master plan for an arts center. Architect Roy Grounds at far left and gallery director Eric Westbrook (third from left) stand with museum staff members and a helmeted construction foreman in the cavernous room, where the state will entertain official guests. Life in this culture-conscious city of 2,270,000 calls for fashionable clothes; leading designers like Norma Tullo often work into the night to meet the demand. Connoisseurs of wine abound: Monday Club members gather in Jimmy Watson's bistro to sip Australian or European vintages, and to make a game of identifying vineyards and years.

TED SPIEGEL, RAPHO GUILLUMETTE

University of Melbourne class of '67 waits in Wilson Hall to receive degrees from Sir Robert Menzies, K.T., Chancellor of the 14,000-student school and former Prime Minister of Australia. Below, a young father smiles jubilantly after earning a master's in geology. Nobel laureate Sir Macfarlane Burnet (above, standing) and Dr. Gustav Nossal, alumni, conduct immunology research in a University laboratory.

Thoroughbreds on Flemington Course parade at the Melbourne Cup, one of the great handicap races of the

In top hats and morning coats, members of the Victoria Racing Club, sponsor of the November classic for more than one hundred years, chat outside their stand at the track. For them and thousands of other horse fanciers, *Cup Day* includes a pre-race picnic of champagne and chicken. Fans in the enclosures expectantly raise binoculars as starting time approaches. For a stake in this $60,000 run, bettors throughout Australia queue up at official ticket windows. The attractive visitor opposite may find herself in a competition of a different sort: "Fashions in the Field." Judges choose chic entries from the crowd for a hat-and-dress contest held after the race.

TED SPIEGEL, RAPHO GUILLUMETTE

world. After the walk-by, all work stops as the nation fixes its attention on the two-mile run over the turf.

"Carols by Candlelight:" Lifting their voices amid a softly flickering constellation, 20,000 carolers sit in and around Melbourne's Sidney Myer Music Bowl on Christmas Eve. Orchestra and choir perform under an acre-size canopy fashioned of aluminum-covered wood panels and supported by steel masts and a web of cables. Funds for the amphitheater came from the Sidney Myer Charity Trust in memory of Australia's most famous department store magnate, a Russian immigrant who began his career in Melbourne as a peddler in 1899. Since opening in 1959, the Bowl has offered free concerts, operas, ballets, and a variety of other cultural events.

Australia's capital, Canberra affords the spaciousness and beauty of a park for the national government. In gleaming Parliament House, the legislature has met since moving from Melbourne in 1927. Prime Minister John Grey Gorton, above, confers in Government House with his Deputy, John McEwen, and the Rt. Hon. Lord Casey, Governor-General (extreme left). Across Lake Burley Griffin, named for the Chicago architect who planned the city, Anzac Parade leads to the domed War Memorial. Bronze wall panels there record the names of 101,849 Australians who died in overseas wars.

DAVID MOORE, BLACK STAR (BOTTOM), AND NATIONAL GEOGRAPHIC PHOTOGRAPHER WINFIELD PARKS

Growing power source: Sparks erupt as Ensio Sipponen touches grinder to rough pipe at Murray 2 power station, one of seven in the Snowy Mountains Hydro-electric Scheme. Now three-quarters realized, the project calls for 16 large dams around 7,310-foot Mount Kosciusko, the continent's highest peak, to harness seven rivers for power and for irrigation. In Tumut 2 machine hall, technicians inspect generators that produce peak-load electricity for Canberra, Melbourne, and Sydney. Glassed openings show natural rock 800 feet underground. Blowering Dam (below) nears completion as fill tumbles from trucks amid billowing dust. Bulldozers and rollers spread rock and pack the dam's earth core; spraying helps settle the material.

Trailing powdery snow dust after each high-speed turn, a skier sweeps down Back Perisher Mountain in brilliant midday sun, and a vacationist (below) pushes cross-country under an arch of twisted snow eucalypts. Skiing has boomed to multimillion-dollar proportions since the 1950's, when construction crews for the Snowy Scheme built all-weather roads to previously inaccessible slopes in the Mount Kosciusko area. Now chalets and hotels annually welcome thousands of winter-sports enthusiasts, mostly from New South Wales and Victoria. From June to October Australia's ski fields, among the world's largest, offer a glistening paradise virtually free of avalanches and ravines.

4

Sydney, Cradle of a Country; Bathurst and Merino Wool

MARY ANN HARRELL

SUNSET GLEAMED on Sydney's Harbour Bridge and the sails of evening
yachts as *Nemesis* swung away from the police boat shed at Dawes Point,
with Constable William Harley at the helm. "We'll cruise around. We
never patrol the same way twice," said Sgt. Gerald Robertson, and we
turned eastward on the calm waters of Port Jackson.

Jerry and Bill pointed out the classic inlets and landmarks from the
days when Australia's history and Sydney's were one. Sydney Cove,
where the First Fleet landed its tired marines and bedraggled convicts in
January, 1788. Bennelong Point, where the Opera House walls catch
flickering rhythms of shimmer from the tides. Farm Cove, where the
convicts planted their first feeble crops and the Botanic Gardens flourish
now. "There's Government House up there," Jerry said. "The Queen
landed here for her visit in 1954. That had us busy, all right, keeping
private boats at a distance!"

At Rushcutters Bay, with its three marinas, we eased past a flotilla of
pleasure craft at their moorings. By now lights shone from the apartment
blocks alongshore. A narrow glow rippled near one cabin cruiser; Jerry
commented, "Somebody's living on board, commuting to work by dinghy."

We rounded Point Piper, one of Sydney's most fashionable addresses.
In Rose Bay our spotlight picked out a flying boat, as quiet as the gulls
perched on her wings. "She may be the last of the old Sunderlands," said

*"The finest harbour in the world," British colonial Governor Arthur Phillip
called the deep, landlocked waterway he chose in 1788 for Australia's first
settlement. Now a burgeoning city of 2,600,000 people, and capital of New
South Wales, Sydney stands as the country's largest city and chief port of entry.*

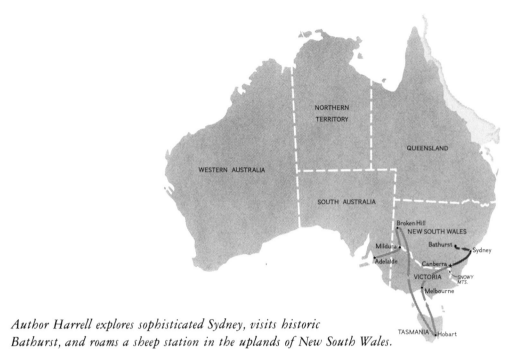

NORTHERN TERRITORY

QUEENSLAND

WESTERN AUSTRALIA

SOUTH AUSTRALIA

Broken Hill
NEW SOUTH WALES

Mildura
Bathurst
Sydney

Adelaide
Canberra

VICTORIA
SNOWY MTS.

Melbourne

TASMANIA
Hobart

Author Harrell explores sophisticated Sydney, visits historic Bathurst, and roams a sheep station in the uplands of New South Wales.

Bill. "Ex-New Zealand Air Force. They take mail and tourists out to Lord Howe Island, 430 miles east."

Nemesis tossed her way along as we approached the Heads. "She's only 45 feet," said Jerry, "but she's our favorite if somebody needs a rescue out on the Pacific." He laughed. "We don't have a federal Coast Guard like yours; there's nobody to rescue *us*. The Volunteer Coastal Patrol helps. It's made up of private powerboats. We put a uniformed man on some of them for Boxing Day—the Sydney-Hobart yacht race, you know. Then you see *everything* out, even canoes, and surfboards with chaps paddling away like ducks."

Once we eased under Spit Bridge and up Middle Harbour, the glow of city lights dimmed. Here, near the center of a metropolitan area that covers more than 670 square miles, waterside homes look out on channels sheltered by tree-darkened hills. Naturally enough we talked of weekends: sailing, swimming, football. Australia is shirt-sleeves country, first-name country, and above all weekend country. Bill told me about his suburb on the North Shore. "We've got a good surf beach; we've got bush not far away, at Frenchs Forest. I get home and get on my shorts and T-shirt and thong sandals and that's me; then I'm right."

We met the workaday world again on our way back: a prawning boat with two white lights to say "trawl nets out," a freighter at anchor waiting to clear quarantine. About 4,000 ships, from interstate coasters to seagoing tramps, call each year. We ran under the Harbour Bridge to check on the docks beyond.

In Darling Harbour new wharves and sheds go up as the Maritime Services Board brings the port up to date. "They're dredging these channels for the new bulk carriers from Japan," explained Jerry. We turned into White Bay, at Balmain, where new terminals will serve container vessels for faster loading. Sydney's exports of wheat, coal, and oil rise from year to year. The total shipping volume reached more than five million tons in 1966-67 and included not only wool but manufactured goods as well; cars, trucks, machinery of all sorts. Our discussion had turned to trade and immigration—universal topics—when two sharp pings on the radio alerted us for a call: "Launch *Nemesis,* return to the boat shed...." A quiet night for the harbor, always the heart of the city.

On weekday mornings and evenings, commuters cross the water: eight lanes of peak-hour traffic on the bridge, crowds on the green ferries that scurry from Sydney Cove to the North Shore. Traffic keeps to the left, of course; in narrow downtown streets it keeps a slow pace as Holdens and Toyotas and Fords jostle around green double-decker buses. Along the footpaths—sidewalks, that is—pedestrians step out briskly. With about 2,600,000 people, Sydney gives Australia a byword for bustle.

A spirited mixture of buildings gives the city a try-it-on air: Georgian composure on Macquarie Street, with St. James' Church and the State Parliament House; Victorian pomp in older banks and commercial buildings; Wild West practicality in overhangs that protect shoppers from the brilliant sun; British practicality in shopping arcades; and pure up-to-date gusto in skyscrapers.

Now that ceramic tile covers the shells of the Opera House, their white gleam strikes fresh as the afternoon wind from the sea. "The building's about 50 percent complete," Charles Weatherburn, a senior architect, told me, "and the name's a complete misnomer, because this will be a center for all the performing arts. We'll also have multilingual translation equipment for international conventions of 3,000—a southeast Asia conference of engineers, for example." I had not heard of this feature before, and Mr. Weatherburn said it would be "entirely new for Australia."

F OR THAT MATTER, I had not expected Sydney's delightful jumble of trees—exotic imports from England; pines; eucalypts; palms. And I had not expected the fountains that set forth new ways of playing with water. In the Botanic Gardens, trim dark jets give a disciplined briskness to a war memorial. At the Colonial Sugar Refining Company building, water slips down a translucent monolith of glass darker than emerald. Rings of spray dance silver by day and golden by night in the El Alamein Memorial Fountain, at Kings Cross—unless teen-agers tint it red or blue with food coloring, or fling in detergent to make volcanoes of suds. Peak-hour traffic backs up at the Cross, but—as people told me with a note of pride—the scene swings through the day and late into the night.

"Have you seen the Cross?" Sydneysiders ask. "You must, that's where the action is." To beards and beads, the local hippies add suntan and smiles. Girls in minute miniskirts and patterned stockings parade past the espresso houses. Friends guided me to a cellar restaurant with carpet-bag steak—stuffed with oysters, and excellent—and a 14th-floor restaurant with unequaled chocolate mousse and a sweeping view of the city.

Australians and Americans who know both cities compare Sydney to San Francisco, citing hilly streets, distinctive atmosphere, a majestic bridge for a great harbor, miles of coast for a playground.

I found out why Sydney boasts of surf beaches, plural: Its forceful sandstone headlands screen one sand-rimmed crescent from another and contribute to the rip currents that can sweep away even the strongest swimmer. Warren Moore of the Manly Surf Life Saving Club kept an eye on his stretch of shore as he explained the work of his fellow volunteers. "We have 12 patrols, 9 to 12 men each, that take turns of duty on Saturday afternoons, Sundays, and public holidays." He showed me the surfboat, and the reel for lines that secure a "beltman" who swims out in emergencies. "Some people you rescue just say, 'I'm all right.' They're embarrassed; they know they were in trouble. Later they send in money with a note, 'Thanks for bringing me in.'"

On Sundays, Australian families spend hours together. Within 20 miles of downtown Sydney, they can explore the sandstone bush country of Ku-ring-gai Chase, a state national park. At its fauna sanctuary, emus pace about with the splay-footed poise of dinosaurs. Keeper Ian Scott thoughtfully roused an indolent wombat for me. "Mate, you have a lady visitor here," he said. It trundled over, badgerlike, to get its ears scratched. Kangaroos lolled in the sun, propped on an elbow with the grace of a Parisian marquise in her boudoir.

Conservationists and graziers argue the future of roos, especially the red species. In Canberra, Dr. Harry Frith, Chief of the Division of Wildlife Research, CSIRO, had told me some conclusions from his pioneer ecological studies and those of his colleagues. "Kangaroos do compete with sheep to an extent, but the diets differ enough that a range could support both. Kangaroos can flourish on poorer pastures, producing more protein than domestic stock; they're a valuable food resource." And he added, "We want our children to be able to go out and see our own animals in their own country."

NONE OF THIS COUNTRY has yielded easily to man. I learned the landscape of the first settlement with the internationally known writer Olaf Ruhen of Sydney. From waterside streets he evoked the mangroves tangling the eastern side of Sydney Cove, great outcrops of eroded sandstone on the western shore, still known as the Rocks. On that peninsula, convicts huddled under guard, sheltered by caves and ledges until they finished their huts. As we rambled among old houses and pubs in the shadow of the Harbour Bridge, Olaf related stories of the rough years of whaling and the exploits of larrikin mobs—gangs, or city bushrangers in effect—that intimidated the town in the 1870's and '80's. Now, it seems, progress may turn this unvarnished area into a forest of skyscrapers.

The Hon. Robin William Askin, Premier of New South Wales, emphasized the speed of change as he turned from his office window, with its harbor view: "It started right down there, only 180 years ago. In only two long lifetimes all this has grown from nothing." In the midst of a political campaign, he had some nonpartisan explanations of Australian democracy. "You'll find differences in our parties from state to state. For instance, New South Wales is the most heavily industrialized state; we account for about 45 percent of primary and secondary production in the nation. Naturally this affects our politics. Since World War II the distance

Sydney in the 1880's: "The overflow of bricks and mortar has spread like a lava flood," wrote an English visitor. Made prosperous by a busy port, the century-old city boasted railways and suburbs — and a third of a million people.

between our parties has grown less. This is partly because many of the things Labor stood for — shorter hours, better pay — have been secured. The Liberal Party has played its part in encouraging social gains, and has moved much closer to the center."

I asked about compulsory voting. "It came in back in the 1920's, and I believe everyone takes it for granted," he replied. "We think it makes every citizen especially aware of his responsibility — or hers." And if the voter has no preference? "Oh, he can write a big X across the paper and that won't count for any candidate. He may even add a rude remark if he wants to; the ballot is secret, of course. The important thing is that he can keep a government in power, or he can turn it out. That's democratic."

A written constitution, American style, and trust in precedents, English style, meet in Australia's federal system. Sir Garfield Barwick, Chief Justice of Australia, outlined these distinctions when I met him in chambers off Taylor Square. "Our judicial system is somewhat different to yours. The state courts administer the federal law. The High Court, which is the Supreme Court of Australia, acts as the final court of appeal for each state; we sit in turn in each of the state capitals — we shall be in Melbourne tomorrow. The High Court decides constitutional cases as your Supreme Court does, but not so many. Australia has no Bill of Rights in

73

the Constitution." As in Britain, he said, "everyone seems to know what's expected and assumes that our basic principles will be followed."

Free speech flourishes in the Domain on Sunday afternoons. I strolled through the 125-acre park, on high ground above Farm Cove, and stopped near an anarchist's black-and-red flag as he proclaimed, "I am a citizen of the world!" A heckler interrupted: "I think it's a wonderful thing we have this kind of country so we can listen to these idiots, these galahs." (Galahs make more racket than other parrots. And I overheard the Aussie term for a crackpot: "He's a ratbag.") Citizens with blunt questions and half-eaten ice cream surrounded a man who denounced the "warlords of America." Suntanned blokes interrupted a pallid young National Socialist with a sardonic drawl of "Ahh, you're gorgeous!"

Just off the Domain stands the Art Gallery of New South Wales, with Aboriginal art, displays from Polynesia and Melanesia, contemporary Australian work. Sydney attracts painters — full-time or weekend — and an unsung canvas can find a place on the walls of Jim Buckley's pub, the Hotel Newcastle. Here the beer-drinkers might include graziers in from their stations, a parachutist, a colonel in mufti, a TV star from London, a pretty model from Perth, students from everywhere, journalists, art dealers looking for new talent. "When a 16-year-old sells his first picture, it really gives him a lift." Pleasure echoes in Jim's voice.

After this easy-going sociable place, Admiralty House strikes a formal note. Flowerbeds and lawns rival any in England; indoors, drawn curtains mute the southern sun. Here, in an office with Aboriginal bark paintings on the wall and a corncob pipe on the desk, I met His Excellency the Rt. Hon. Lord Casey, Governor-General of Australia — official representative of Her Majesty the Queen, and completely representative of his countrymen in hospitality.

"I've known the people of quite a number of countries," he said, "and I've never known any other two who hit it off together like Australians and Americans. They're like the two blades of a pair of scissors. This has always been true, in my experience." That experience began in 1913, proving especially valuable in 1940 when Richard Gardiner Casey opened Australia's first diplomatic mission in Washington, D. C.

He summarized his role as representative of the Sovereign with the observation: "It's hard to define, really; there's nothing like it in your system." He made little of purely ceremonial duties such as presiding at the opening of Parliament, and emphasized matters of state. Like the Queen, the Governor-General has the right to be consulted, the right to encourage, and the right to warn. No legislation becomes law until he signs it; he reads all important official papers and diplomatic dispatches, discussing them with the Ministers concerned.

The third Australian citizen to fill this post of honor, Lord Casey remembers his childhood glimpses of the grandfather who had served as surgeon and magistrate for the penal settlement at Port Arthur in the 1830's. His own public service includes combat at Gallipoli, nine years as Minister for External Affairs, and a decade in charge of CSIRO.

Lord Casey gave me an unforgettable picture of his country today in a conversation that ranged over many aspects of Australian life. It ended with his thoughtful verdict: "We've been lucky."

Lucky—and tough. Even a gentle region calls for struggle. On the 40-minute flight from Sydney to Bathurst, I watched the Blue Mountains glide below the wing—hauntingly like the Appalachians until scarps of sandstone break the hazy slopes of bush. Convicts in black-and-yellow stripes completed the first road across these ranges in 1815; brick soon replaced turf huts at Bathurst. But as long as bullock drays hauled every item in trade, only two commodities would earn a profit on 50-mile journeys: wool—or gold.

Today Bathurst balances secondary industry against agriculture—precision engineering, shoe factories, a cannery, against vegetable growing, orchards, wheat. This town of 17,500 people, of low buildings on low hills, deals in cattle, wool, and prime lambs. A mob of sheep choked the highway as I arrived, and stock auctioneer Brent Livermore told me why. Drought had driven them out in search of forage. "A grazier may have invested $6 per head in feed already," he said, "and have to sell them at $1 apiece."

IN AN AVERAGE YEAR Brent may handle sales of more than six million dollars. He chanted a sample offer for me, and his wife Mary warned, "If you blink an eye at an auction, you'll be landed with a pen of sheep." Buyers waggle a finger or raise an eyebrow as the bids rise. "They're professionals," Brent said. "I'm working for the vendor, to get him the best price I can. He's entrusted me with his livelihood—with paying for his car, say, or his child's education. I can't think of a more fascinating job."

New South Wales produces 40 percent of Australia's wool clip, and I saw one of its most progressive stations. Gordon Bullock of Bathurst drove me along paved roads and the dirt track across "Mount Horrible" (nicknamed for bumpy riding), to the Thompson property called Warrie: 9,978 acres. As a member of both shire and county councils, Brian Thompson enjoys public affairs—providing roads, footpaths, tax relief for elderly pensioners. But improving Warrie means a struggle against rabbits and weeds, rising costs and wobbly wool prices. "In 1966 we got 57.5 cents a pound for Merino, 48.5 cents in 1967," Brian said.

After a lunch of cold lamb, garden vegetables, Warrie butter, and local honey, we drove down past a stream and on to rolling uplands, opening and closing gates of the rabbitproof fences. I learned how Brian builds up a paddock. Using bulldozers, his hired men knock over the green timber, leaving a few good trees for shade. They stack the useless trunks into heaps for burning. That day I smelled the tang of gum-tree smoke. All the blackberry patches must be poisoned. "See those bushes?" Brian pointed grimly. "There're *hundreds* of rabbits in there."

Casually imported for game in 1859, 24 English wild rabbits multiplied into billions. By 1900 rabbits had invaded all the major sheep-grazing areas of the continent. "They're the greatest scourge in primary industry," Brian said coldly. "In the old days you would see great moving masses of them; they would eat the ground bare. Now the myxomatosis virus limits the numbers, but the only way to have a good pasture is to kill every last single rabbit in it. We use poisoned carrots. Rabbits never give the good grasses a chance to reseed."

Brian adds superphosphate to cleared paddocks and then sows grasses and clovers. "The second year, your paddock carries twice as many sheep." During frequent stops, he taught me the leaves of rye grass, white clover, cock's foot, sub clover, *Phalaris,* all brownish with drought. He picked up a tan seedpod. "Here's the beauty of improved pasture. Sheep can eat the seeds and get some nutriment when land looks perfectly bare." He broke out a black pellet smaller than a peppercorn. "See how you like it. It's sub clover." A pleasant nutty flavor eluded naming. Brian stood up and gazed at the hills around us. Then he said quietly: "Men with unimproved pasture ran out of feed months ago. If we don't get rain we're *settled."*

We inspected a small bark-roofed house in the style of pioneer days, built in Brian's childhood as a playhouse. Two adults would crowd it. As the sun went low, we drove up to a wooded hill and scuffed through eucalyptus bark to look at the "diggers' holes" that riddle this country, relics of the gold rush that began in 1851.

We moved a layer of branches that would support unwary sheep and stared into a shadowy pit, just big enough for a man to dig in while his partner tended a windlass and searched the bucket-loads for metal. "That was doing it the hard way," said Brian, and we turned to leave.

ON THE WAY to Sydney's international airport, the sandy-haired taxi driver pointed out gaily painted old terrace houses above a grass bank that held a red-and-white rowboat, sunflowers, and a corn patch. "Maltese live there," he explained. An accent I could not place lay behind his Australian words with a long I for a long A. He told me where other New Australians have gathered in Sydney: Italians, Greeks, Letts. He thought his story might belong in a book, but not his name.

"I left Hungary in 1945. I was 16 — I was lucky to be alive. My family bombed out, all killed. I went with my school sweetheart — her family all killed. We came to Australia in 1950; yes, we married, three lovely kids. My oldest son is 17, entering the University of New South Wales this year. He plans to be a doctor, since he was 12."

As we edged through the traffic I thought of the country I was, reluctantly, leaving — an immigrant country for most of its history. In less than three decades, more than 1,600,000 migrants have settled in Australia, including some 300,000 refugees. They find the traditional opportunities: the chance of prosperity, the guarantee of freedom. Today they change Australian life even as they adapt to it, behind the counters of delicatessens or the desks of CSIRO.

"Now, we stop here" — a polite summons to the present. We stepped out into the sunlight; he set down the suitcase; he stopped to wave goodbye. "Thank you," he called; *"bon voyage!"*

Houses with red tile roofs, characteristic of Australian suburbs, march along the outskirts of Sydney. Widespread clay deposits provide material for the roofing.

Concrete shells of the new
Sydney Opera House arch
above Bennelong Point, near
the spot where settlers first
stepped ashore. The struc-
ture's shape blends with
billowing spinnakers of 18-
footers racing on Sydney
Harbour. Inside, perform-
ing halls will accommodate
music and ballet, exhibits
and conventions. Beyond
the building, the Harbour
Bridge vaults a narrows
to the city's North Shore.

DAVID MOORE, BLACK STAR (LOWER LEFT), AND NATIONAL GEOGRAPHIC PHOTOGRAPHER WINFIELD PARKS

Red streamers of light trace the flow of traffic on William Street toward Kings Cross —Sydney's Greenwich Village—where the El Alamein Memorial Fountain (above) commemorates Australians who served in the World War II battle in Africa. Floodlit by night, the fountain gleams like a beacon for crowds patronizing bars and coffee shops in the Kings Cross area. Row houses in nearby Paddington soared in value when artists and architects revamped them and painted them in pastel hues.

Sunday in Sydney: Taking their afternoon leisure, Sydney-siders hear an orator in the Domain, one of the city's largest parks. His topic—"Aussies are Awful Lovers"—produces varying reactions in his audience: Two young girls seem intrigued; a man of another generation listens attentively. Each weekend speakers mount makeshift platforms to declaim on subjects ranging from poetry to politics, from rugby to religion. In nearby Hyde Park a chess expert (opposite above) takes on a string of earnest challengers as the gallery watches in thoughtful silence. Wearing a sweater against cool afternoon breezes, a visitor (opposite below) pauses for an ice cream cone on the edge of the park's Archibald Memorial Fountain.

83

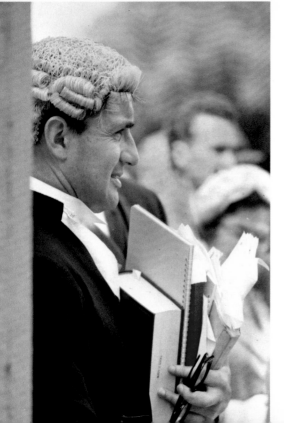

Springtime revelers gaily disregard traffic arrows in downtown Sydney during the annual Waratah Festival, a week-long fête that coincides with the blossoming of the unofficial state flower of New South Wales, the crimson waratah. Antique autos—licensed in Australia as "veteran cars"—bear merrymakers in Saturday's parade, high point of the October festivities. Costumed girls wave from the door of an electric tram; the Mad Hatter draws delighted squeals. A clear sky supports the country's claim as the "Sunshine Continent." Near the city's courts, a bewigged barrister (left) crosses Queens Square. His traditional attire reflects the country's historical link with Britain; even today Australians of British descent account for 90 percent of the population. In Kings Cross, a poodle (opposite right) waits patiently as its owner chats with another shopper.

NATIONAL GEOGRAPHIC PHOTOGRAPHER WINFIELD PARKS

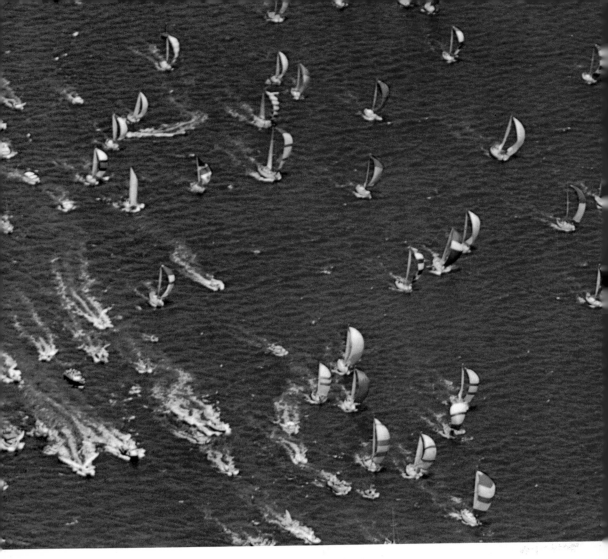

Like skittering water bugs, sailing yachts jockey for position among spectator boats at the start of the 735-mile Sydney-to-Hobart race. Because of frequent high winds, seasoned skippers call the course the world's

NATIONAL GEOGRAPHIC PHOTOGRAPHER WINFIELD PARKS

roughest. The event, begun each year on December 26, normally lasts four or five days, but bad weather can stretch it by a day or more. Below, weekend sailors run before the wind on spacious Sydney Harbour.

At water's edge on Sydney's Bondi Beach a sturdy toddler clutches a paddle held by her mother; to the north, at Manly Beach, Scout Leaders nap in the sun. On hot afternoons as many as 20,000 people converge on these two stretches of sand. Altogether, the city boasts 24 beaches. Small coves shelter some; others reach unbroken for miles.

Bronzed lifeguards on Manly Beach march during a surf carnival, a competition of precision drill and pageantry among clubs of the Surf Life Saving Association of Australia. Volunteers number 25,000, and

DAVID MOORE, BLACK STAR (ABOVE), AND NATIONAL GEOGRAPHIC PHOTOGRAPHER WINFIELD PARKS

rescue some 5,000 swimmers a year. They patrol beaches like the one below, where a sunbather dozes and surfers shoot to shore. When a team spots a bather in trouble, one man swims out with a line; then his partners reel in the two of them. In heavy surf lifeguards launch a five-man boat and row out to the victim.

89

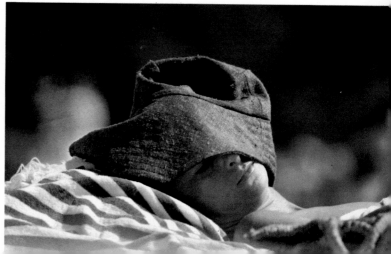

Industrial complex of Port Kembla—Australia's Pittsburgh—sprawls
within sight of its power source, the coal-rich Illawarra Range.
Furnaces here annually produce four million tons of steel,
more than half of the country's total output.

DAVID MOORE, BLACK STAR

NATIONAL GEOGRAPHIC PHOTOGRAPHER WINFIELD PARKS

Harvesting with a barge, waterborne farmers collect sticks of mature rock oysters in the Hawksbury River, 30 miles north of Sydney. Seeding of the crop begins soon after the summer spawning season, when aquiculturists submerge slats over breeding grounds near the river's mouth. Young oysters—called spat (opposite right)—cling to the thin strips for the first six months of their lives; then growers move them upstream to less salty water. After the mollusks have aged three to four years, harvesters chip them off the sticks (right). Sorting and grading (opposite left) end the process; most of the delicacies go to Sydney and Melbourne. Oyster growers along the coast of New South Wales lease their tidal farms from the state for 15-year periods.

Mustering a mob of Merinos, sheepman Brian Thompson carries a lamb on his 9,978-acre Warrie station in New South Wales. Five hands and their dogs help him manage 14,000 sheep and 800 cattle. Rabbitproof fencing protects 250-acre paddocks. Leaving his wife Janet at home, Thompson sets out by motorcycle to inspect a hilly pasture; daughter Vicky rides part way.

95

5

Queensland: Gold in the Hills And Gold Along the Beach

HECTOR HOLTHOUSE

WHENEVER I COME BACK to Queensland from any other state, I always relax a little. The tempo is slower here. I am a Queenslander, and I like it that way. I notice this change of mood with the first view of our capital from the air.

Brisbane sprawls out lazily over a wide valley, tall buildings at its heart, several clusters of ships at wharves on the winding Brisbane River, red-tiled or tin-roofed houses spreading out in regular patterns toward surrounding bush and farmland.

On a particular occasion in February, 1968, I gazed through the plane window with more critical eyes than usual. I was returning from Sydney, where I had been asked to write this chapter; I was trying to look at the city I live in just as a visitor might. Naturally, I recognized familiar landmarks as the Boeing 727 banked downriver toward Eagle Farm Airport. To the south, smoking chimneys marked the Brisbane abattoir with its vast complex of saleyards and holding-paddocks for cattle. Beef is my state's largest single export commodity; with allied products, it brings in more than $100 million a year. At either side of the river mouth rose a refinery; crude oil comes to them through a 186-mile-long pipeline from Australia's first commercial field, the wells at Moonie.

Eagle Farm Airport is unimpressive. Its igloo hangars held American planes in World War II, when Gen. Douglas MacArthur made his

With a warm smile and a friendly note, a Meter Maid comes to the rescue of an overdue parker at Surfers Paradise, a seaside resort on the 20-mile-long Gold Coast of Queensland. The local merchants' Progress Association employs the girls to place coins in expired meters; the card goes on the car's windshield.

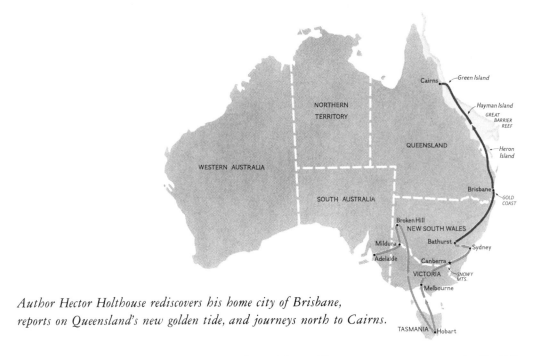

NORTHERN TERRITORY

QUEENSLAND

WESTERN AUSTRALIA

SOUTH AUSTRALIA

Cairns
Green Island

Hayman Island
GREAT BARRIER REEF

Heron Island

Brisbane
GOLD COAST

Broken Hill
NEW SOUTH WALES

Mildura

Bathurst
Sydney

Adelaide

Canberra

VICTORIA
SNOWY MTS.

Melbourne

TASMANIA
Hobart

Author Hector Holthouse rediscovers his home city of Brisbane,
reports on Queensland's new golden tide, and journeys north to Cairns.

headquarters in Brisbane. They still serve as temporary terminal buildings — and signs of progress. In January, 1968, the state could report more than 200 major development projects under way or announced, representing a total investment of $1,405 million. That left no money to spare for a new airport. Development comes first in Queensland today. The state is in the midst of its greatest boom since the gold rush of a century ago.

I thought of the gold rush while driving into the city; the road runs along the northern riverbank and its high slopes have been one of Brisbane's most sought-after residential areas for a hundred years. Colonial-style homes — old brown or white single-story wooden houses with long verandas commanding the whole reach of the river — spread with indolent dignity. Now high, tight-knit apartment blocks, in yellow or cream brick and pastel concrete, have encroached on once-wide lawns. The best of the two styles symbolize Queensland's two peaks of prosperity — the gold rush of yesteryear and the industrial boom of today.

Nearly all these buildings, old and new alike, stand clear of the ground, either on wooden piles — stumps, we call them — or on concrete piers. Brisbane's summer-day temperatures range through the 80's and 90's, and builders have always tried to catch the river breezes.

In spite of new construction on every side, the business district has an air of dusty shabbiness, caused mainly by temporary boardings around construction sites and all the grit and clatter of bulldozers, cranes, and concrete mixers. For ten years I have watched Brisbane bursting at the seams. Fighting a losing battle against the planners are the city's old trams, or streetcars. For years they ground their way along the middle of the main streets, a symbol of Queensland's determination not to be hurried. Now diesel buses are gradually replacing them.

The average Brisbanite takes all the changes with his usual unruffled calm. The first thing I noticed that day when I got off the plane was that the people, as always, seemed to move a little more slowly, that they were not quite so intent on what they were doing, and that they were more inclined than people in other places to stop and exchange a few words as they went about their work.

The friendliness of Queenslanders is tradition throughout Australia, but many of them—particularly if no strangers are present—will tell you that this tradition is the Great Australian Myth. As a rule, the Queenslander takes things quietly and rarely asks questions unless you make it clear you want him to. He does, however, feel a genuine concern for your welfare and comfort. You feel this most strongly in the outback.

In early 1966 I was up north in the Cape York Peninsula, collecting material for a book on the Palmer River gold rush of the 1870's. I followed a dirt track through dozens of creeks and rivers, all of which had to be forded. I edged the car through one creek crossing nearly too deep for it. Then I noticed, in the shade of a clump of paperbark trees, an Aboriginal stockman in the usual broad-brimmed hat, khaki shirt and trousers, and elastic-sided riding boots. He was squatting beside his campfire. I pulled up and strolled across to ask him about the crossings along the road.

"You'll be right as far as Laura [the next town]," he told me. "I've just made a billy of tea."

We squatted beside the fire, talking and taking turns sipping scalding-hot tea from his smoke-blackened billy can. My host produced a battered tobacco tin and packet of papers, and began to roll himself a cigarette. I had given up smoking, but the habit is so universal in the outback that a bushman would assume I had run out of tobacco—and in those parts the nearest place to get more can be a couple of days' travel away.

Before I realized what he was thinking the stockman was holding his cigarette out to me, neatly rolled but not gummed down. There was nothing I could do but accept it, run my tongue along the gummed edge of the paper, seal it, and light up from a burning twig. My host began fiddling about with the fire. It was only then that I knew he had given me the last of his tobacco.

QUEENSLAND, sliced out of the northeastern part of the continent, stretches 1,260 miles north from the 29th parallel of south latitude. East of its tropical coastline lies the Great Barrier Reef, 1,250 miles long. The western boundary, except for a northern tableland and coastal strip on the Gulf of Carpentaria, roughly coincides with the limit of profitable occupation. Mountain ranges run north and south, above a narrow coastal plain. They produce, to the east, well-watered farmland, and, to the west, fertile plains that become drier the farther inland you go.

Not long ago I drove out over this country to gather stories of the days when the first settlers were moving out with their cattle. About 80 miles west of Brisbane the road winds up the Great Dividing Range and through a gap to the city of Toowoomba, almost hidden under shade trees. No matter what the season, almost every house is surrounded by a garden ablaze with flowers. The rich loam of the range-top will grow anything. Fertile soil extends for hundreds of square miles, the famous wheat-growing region called the Darling Downs. West of Toowoomba is dairying country—creek flats green with fodder crops, interspersed with hilly, tree-studded grassland.

Within another 100 miles, I could see already the effect of less rainfall. The gum trees are more twisted and the grass is browner, both toughened to meet a harder climate. Wheatfields gradually give way to open forest and grass with flocks of sheep and some cattle.

The land got drier as I drove on. Trees thinned out, became more stunted. Other travelers became scarce. Every mile the sameness grew more oppressive. Farther west and southward lay the Channel Country, a maze of the multiple beds of rivers that run only in the wet season. After the water has been over it the land blooms in a mass of pink and purple flowers, good pasture for cattle. When dry, it is desert.

BACK IN 1824 when the whole of colonial Australia was called New South Wales, the future capital of Queensland was founded as a penal outpost for twice-convicted men—officials thought Sydney jails too comfortable for them. By 1842, when Brisbane had been closed to convicts and opened to free settlers, men who had brought their sheep and cattle north onto the Darling Downs were looking for a seaport. With their trade, Brisbane prospered.

Resenting the rule of faraway Sydney, the graziers joined with Brisbane merchants to press for separation from New South Wales; and in 1859 Queensland, with a population of 23,500 and seven pence halfpenny in the treasury, became a separate colony. Threatened by a depression in 1867, the government offered rewards for the discovery of gold. Within months a man named James Nash found it at a place later named Gympie, north of Brisbane on the Mary River. A horde of 25,000 gold-hungry diggers converged on Gympie, and enough gold came out of the river flats to help put Queensland on its feet.

In the next decade, more new goldfields opened up. Thousands of men poured into country inhabited by warlike Aborigines who had never seen a white man. Hundreds of white men and tribes of Aborigines died in the fighting that followed. Chinese swarmed in until, on parts of the goldfields, they outnumbered Europeans by more than ten to one. In the clashes that resulted were sown some of the seeds of the White Australia Policy that excluded immigrants from Asia.

As Queensland's golden tide was reaching its flood, agriculture was creeping up the fertile coast. Sugar-cane planters imported South Sea islanders—called Kanakas—to do the heavy work. By the time the golden tide had begun to ebb, sugar lands reached north of Cairns and the industry was well established. It had become the mainstay of tropical Queensland when federal legislation introduced the White Australia Policy and ordered the Kanakas sent home.

When I took my first job as a chemist in a sugar mill near Mackay a few years before World War II, sugar men were still conscious of the frontier they were holding, and when we put sugar in our tea or coffee we always took an extra spoonful "to support the industry." Gangs of tough men were still cutting cane with broad-bladed knives. They would labor in the

Careened for repairs, Capt. James Cook's stricken vessel, H. M. Bark Endeavour, *lies beached near the site of present-day Cooktown after striking a reef. Crewmen in a pinnace seek a shoal-free channel. On his 1770 voyage, the famed explorer charted the east coast of Australia and claimed its entire length for Britain.*

fields all day under the broiling sun and fill the pubs on Friday pay nights. When the season ended, about December, they would go south to the cities—like the diggers before them—to live it up on their earnings.

Today more than half of Queensland's 17-million-ton sugar crop is harvested by machinery. Although cane cutters of the old tough breed are becoming scarcer, the type shows no signs of dying out. All over the country, big construction projects need such men.

A young cousin of mine named Richard—one of a family of seven with a small farm to support them—felt the call a few years ago. Aged 17, he went south and took a job driving a bulldozer on the Snowy Scheme. For more than a year his family had received nothing from him but a few non-committal notes. Then, at Christmas, the blast of a motor horn startled everyone in the farmhouse. Rushing to the door, they saw Richard at the wheel of a brand-new Chrysler. He had come back, he said, to take his whole family for a holiday to the Gold Coast. While they were away, he would pay another family to look after the farm. And that was exactly what he did.

Richard's choice of a gift is typical of the new industrial Australia. A holiday on the Gold Coast—many still call it Surfers, after Surfers

Paradise, its principal town—has become a symbol of success, a sign that one has made the grade. Exactly how this happened, no one really knows. I saw it happen, and I still wonder how much of it was an accident. The Gold Coast fills a narrow strip of ocean foreshore extending 20 miles to the New South Wales border. I recall it in the late 1930's, a string of easy-going holiday towns joined by a broad, white-sand beach and a narrow road. During the postwar decade, these towns lazed their way along as Queensland's population grew and Brisbane attracted manufacturers. The men who brought the factories discovered these resorts, particularly Surfers. They saw a future in the long white sand strip and began to buy pieces of it. Suddenly its fortunes went up like a rocket.

I remember Christmas of 1959, when the old bitumen road from Brisbane was packed with cars crawling along bumper-to-bumper at 20 miles an hour or less. The towns were crowded to capacity. Caravans and tents filled all the camping areas. New hotels, shops, and blocks of flats were not nearly enough to hold visitors.

Once again Queensland had struck gold—not in the hills this time, but down on the beach. There was an exuberant feeling of money in the air. One morning I watched two garbage collectors emptying cans into their truck. They wore the usual dress—shirt, shorts, and boots—but, in addition, each wore a tall, shining, silk top hat.

Today the Gold Coast is growing, literally month by month, and establishing itself ever more firmly as an institution. Most Australian workers get at least 3 weeks' vacation every year, and 13 weeks' long-service leave after 15 years with the same employer. And many vacationists want to spend their holidays in the sun.

O F ALL THE GREAT INDUSTRIAL DEVELOPMENTS that have changed the face of Queensland during the past five years, those of Gladstone are the most spectacular. Early in 1958, I motored through the sleepy town, seaport for a beef- and coal-producing hinterland. When I saw it next, late one Friday pay night in 1966, the town had trebled its size, and almost every second man in its crowded streets and hotel bars was wearing that unofficial badge of the construction worker, a yellow safety helmet.

In March, 1968, Mayor W. R. Golding announced plans for the year. The harbor would handle 7 million tons of Moura coal for Japan. In addition, 1.8 million tons of bauxite would arrive from Weipa, on the Gulf of Carpentaria, and 900,000 tons of alumina would be exported by Queensland Alumina Ltd. Plants for sulphuric acid, fertilizer, and mineral sand would soon be started. Obviously the coming Christmas will see many eyes turned from Gladstone toward that holiday on the Gold Coast.

Other travelers will be considering a visit to the Great Barrier Reef and the coastal islands. My first acquaintance with those waters came before World War II. With friends, I used to sail out to rocky islands about ten miles from shore and in half an hour we would collect from the rocks all the oysters we could eat.

My favorite holiday spot is Heron Island, about 44 miles offshore from

Gladstone. When I first went there, after the war, I saw it at its best—in late October. The great green turtles were coming ashore to lay their eggs, and the migratory wedge-tailed shearwaters, better known locally as muttonbirds, were nesting in burrows under the tall pisonia trees. Their burrows were so thick in the sand that I could hardly walk without putting a foot through one, and at night their cries sounded like a thousand infant children in distress. In the branches of the pisonias, the white-capped noddies were nesting in thousands; and one day I found, hidden away in the heart of a thick clump of pandanus trees, the nest of a heron, that shy, rarely seen bird from which the island gets its name.

Only on islands like Heron can you see the coral gardens and their sea animals properly, unless you are a skin diver. I used to walk over the reef, following the tide out across coral platforms. On the sandy bottoms of the pools lie starfish of various species; their colors are harsh and crude, like the bags of bluing for old-fashioned washing days and the bright brick-red sands of the Central Australian plains. The fishes range from about 12 inches in length to glittering specks. They vary from sleek torpedoes to chunks of colored movement that caricature every basic shape of a fish. Slugs the hue of raw meat undulate and cavort in the water with a grace no dancer ever dreamed of. The rising tide drives you back to the shore trying to remember all you have seen, and knowing you will never retain more than a fraction of it.

As recently as 1968 I had never seen the north's main tourist area, the Cumberland group—high, rocky islands about 575 miles north of Brisbane. Among them runs the Whitsunday Passage, which Captain Cook discovered on Whit Sunday, 1770. I went out to Hayman Island, northernmost of the Whitsundays, in March. As the launch swung away from land, the tree-clad slopes of the islands rose so high that we seemed to be sailing in a landlocked harbor, with white beaches in sheltered coves. Hayman's fringing reefs shelter water so warm that you can swim at any time of the year, but you must dive to the coral to see it properly.

Fritz Mair, an Aqua-Lung diver who has explored reefs in many parts of the Pacific, calls the underwater life here the most wonderful he has ever seen. "When you swim along," he told me, "about a million fish go with you—just curious. Sometimes, suddenly, you will feel the atmosphere change. Then, zip, all the little fish are gone. You look around. You know what you will see: a shark, or maybe just the shadow of a shark." He has spotted eight sharks at one time; none has attacked him.

Still farther up the coast, I stopped at Green Island, 16 miles offshore from Cairns and the only coral cay except Heron that tourists can reach readily. It offers a grim example of the havoc people can cause by not understanding the delicate balance that governs reef life. For many years collectors came here seeking a beautiful mollusk called the giant triton. So thoroughly did they scour the reef that it almost disappeared.

The giant triton's natural prey is a kind of spiny starfish called the crown-of-thorns. This, in turn, feeds on living coral. With the giant triton gone, the crown-of-thorns multiplied unhindered and its onslaught on the coral was devastating.

When I returned to Brisbane, I discussed the problem with Dr. Robert Endean, Reader in Zoology at the University of Queensland and an authority on the Great Barrier Reef. "The situation is very serious indeed," he said. "Perhaps the only solution will be to import giant tritons, from the Philippines, where they are plentiful." He pointed out threats to the Reef, from crews of many foreign fishing vessels, oil exploration and limestone mining, and stressed the need for a balanced conservation plan.

Meanwhile, fortunately, some of the coral shows regeneration that is restoring one of the main tourist attractions of Cairns. Most northerly of Queensland's cities, Cairns, flanked by green fields of sugar cane and overlooked by jungle-clad mountains, still likes to take life lazily. Its people are friendly, its restaurants among the best in the state, its beer and its sea foods unequaled.

ON MY TRIP NORTH early in 1966, people told me it is only north of Cairns that the real tropics begin. Here the Cook Highway skirts one of the most beautiful stretches of Australia's coastline. On wet, fertile soil, everything grows in profusion—sugar cane on the flats, jungle on the slopes. Flowering trees and shrubs line the road; orchids stud the tree-tops. Quiet beaches shelter small communities whose people like to let the world's bustle go by. In the untouched jungle, wild pigs grow big and sleek on wild mangoes. Large fruit-eating bats—known as flying foxes—gather in hordes; at dusk, I have seen them darken the sky.

The farther north you go, the thicker the jungle becomes. At last, on the south bank of the Daintree River, the road ends. A gravel track has branched off to Cooktown, once a roaring gold-rush seaport, now a shell of its former self. To the west, this Cape York Peninsula region is tough and rocky: the Palmer River country. Here, in the 1870's, 35,000 miners poured in to harvest a million ounces of gold.

Many remained in the district during the '90's. Stan Boyd of Cooktown, alert and active at 78, told me his childhood memories of them. He had plenty of other children to play with, he said. "One couple I remember had 19 children, and that was not exceptional. They lost four in one week and two the next week from diphtheria. Malaria killed a lot of children and adults, too, in those days."

When the miners left, a few cattle stations struggled on. Floods and sodden roads would keep them isolated for weeks and months in the wet season. For three-quarters of a century the peninsula remained nearly as wild as it had been before Europeans came to Australia.

But since early 1966, American investors have bought grazing leases covering more than 15,000 square miles. Some $20 million of American capital has been set aside for new fences and stockyards. In the Cape York Peninsula, developers have leased 7 million acres. The government has begun constructing beef roads. The taming of Queensland's far-distant north is now under way at last.

Using his arms as paddles, a surfer parallels the beach in search of a rolling wave that will speed him back to shore before night falls at Surfers Paradise.

NATIONAL GEOGRAPHIC PHOTOGRAPHER WINFIELD PARKS

Largest river port in Australia, and capital of Queensland, Brisbane shares its name with the broad stream that loops through its heart. Ocean liners and freighters can berth near the center of the city; wharves extend for ten miles downstream. Home to almost half of the 1,718,000 people of the state, Brisbane serves as southern Queensland's major shipping point for sugar, wool, meat, minerals, timber, wheat, and dairy products. The 320-foot-tall clock tower of City Hall looms at left; lights streak the harbor as a ferry shuttles passengers from one side of the city to the other. In shorts and knee socks—summer business attire—a Brisbanite waits for a tram near a uniformed high-school student.

NATIONAL GEOGRAPHIC PHOTOGRAPHER WINFIELD PARKS

Great gray kangaroo at the Lone Pine Sanctuary outside Brisbane keeps protective watch over the 8-month-old joey in her pouch. Only three-quarters of an inch long when born, the tiny marsupial crawls through its mother's fur to get into the pouch and first peeps out when 7 to 8 months old. It lives both in and out of the pouch between the ages of 10 and 11 months, then remains close to the mother until about a year and a half old. With strong, outsize legs, mature roos can bound as far as 26 feet. At left, two half-grown bucks spar playfully with dagger-sharp claws. Furry koalas — marsupials commonly but erroneously called bears — spend most of their time in trees, feeding on eucalyptus leaves. At the Gold Coast's Currumbin Bird Sanctuary, rainbow lorikeets and green scaly-breasted lorikeets eat bits of bread and honey offered by a young admirer.

108

Soaking up November sun, a studious teen-ager basks after a swim. Brief bikinis, unthinkable a generation ago, now find easy acceptance on Australian beaches.

*Relaxed Queenslanders mix
cool draughts and conversation
at a Gold Coast beer garden.
Established in 1959, the City
of Gold Coast has burgeoned
from a string of townships into
the country's foremost vacation
playground. During the peak
season at Christmastime, the
population mushrooms from
53,000 to 150,000 or more.
A visitor taking time from
the sun and the sand orders a
hot dog at a beachside counter.*

111

Cresting wave sweeps precariously balanced youths ashore at Surfers Paradise. A highly disciplined sport, surfing demands superb timing, style—and courage.

ROBERT GOODMAN

Caught by a Fisheye camera lens, trained porpoises leap like graceful circus aerialists at Marineland of Australia, in Surfers Paradise. The mammals jump to grab a braided cord that runs a pennant up a jackstaff. Shaded by checkered bonnets, spectators chat earnestly between acts. At Tweed Heads, just across the border in New South Wales, a porpoise lunges ten feet to snatch a fish from a stick—and the girl who proffered the snack gets a playful nudge from the trainer.

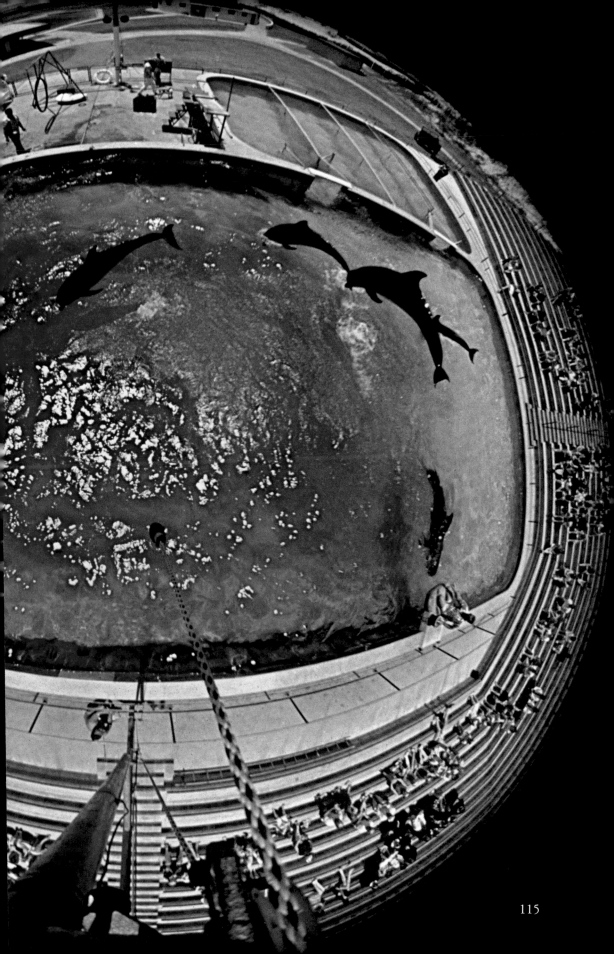

Beachcomber wades the shallows at Green Island, a sand-girt cay of the Great Barrier Reef, earth's mightiest coral rampart. The 1,250-mile-long labyrinth rises from the continental shelf to shield the northeast coast of Australia. Reef waters teem with life. Periscope eyes of the red-mouthed stromb protrude beneath a hairlike growth of algae on its shell. To protect its soft body from predators, a hermit crab makes a home of an abandoned spider shell. The reef heron nests in trees near the water.

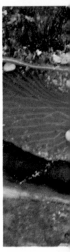

NATIONAL GEOGRAPHIC PHOTOGRAPHER WINFIELD PARKS (TOP AND LOWER LEFT); PAUL A. ZAHL, NATIONAL GEOGRAPHIC STAFF

Harvesting sugar cane, cutters at Innisfail in northern Queensland sever stalks at ground level and lop off the leafy tops. Barefoot workers (opposite) lunch in 90-degree heat at a skid-equipped cane truck. A tractor and trailer haul a loaded truck to a narrow-gauge railway for the trip to a nearby mill where giant rollers will crush out the juice for processing into crystals. Each year mechanical harvesters reap more and more of the crop—60 percent in 1967. Second only to Cuba in the export of raw sugar, Australia ships more than two-thirds of its output to Britain, Japan, the United States, Canada, New Zealand, and Malaysia. The robust Aussie above works in a harvest that totals about 17 million tons of cane a year, on 9,500 farms.

6

Air Bus on a 'Stations Run' From Cairns Into the Outback

BRUCE BRANDER

THE DC-3 WHEELED higher over Cairns. As if ascending a spiral staircase, it circled the sea, as smooth as steel, then again the land still steaming on the cloudy tropical morning.

At 4,000 feet, the twin engines eased from strain to quiet drone. We turned inland. Above jungly coastal mountains, the plane slid in air currents like a car on heavy mud. It settled into smooth movement over the plateau known as the Atherton Tableland.

A "stations run," they call this flight, a weekly link between coastal city, outback towns, and remote cattle stations of the interior. Some 24 people would fit into the long metal tube. But I rode alone, with sacks of onions, crates of oranges, and a truck windshield piled on seats ahead of me, with canned beer and correspondence-school lessons stowed elsewhere on the plane.

The land changed fast, slipping past the rectangular window like a movie. Heavy tropical growth stopped. Open eucalyptus forest took over, parting for fields of food crops. During World War II, thousands of American soldiers and airmen lived on the Tableland, bracing for the threat of Japanese invasion. Now green beans, peanuts, and eight-foot-tall corn grow on the land that they occupied while the Battle of the Coral Sea and other Pacific fighting turned the threat away.

Rainfall diminishes quickly beyond the Great Dividing Range. Just 35

Local government center for cattle country, balconied Carpentaria Shire Council Chambers bakes in the heat of afternoon in Normanton, near Queensland's north coast. Aboriginal stockmen from nearby stations lounge near the plank-floor veranda of the Central Hotel, on the township's wide, deserted main street.

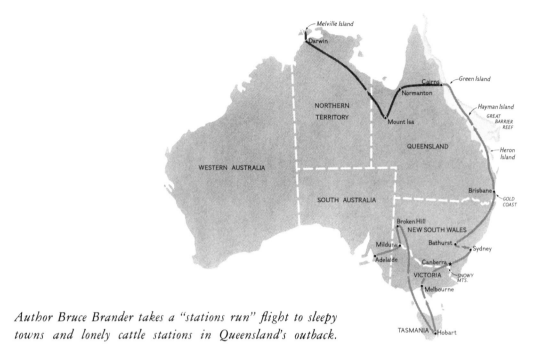

Melville Island
Darwin
Cairns — Green Island
Normanton
Hayman Island
NORTHERN
TERRITORY
GREAT
BARRIER
REEF
Mount Isa
QUEENSLAND
Heron
Island
WESTERN AUSTRALIA
Brisbane
GOLD
COAST
SOUTH AUSTRALIA
Broken Hill
NEW SOUTH WALES
Mildura
Bathurst
Sydney
Adelaide
Canberra
VICTORIA
SNOWY
MTS.
Melbourne
TASMANIA Hobart

Author Bruce Brander takes a "stations run" flight to sleepy towns and lonely cattle stations in Queensland's outback.

minutes off the ground, I saw the effects: russet earth showing between fluffy green treetops, hard blue sky just ahead. With updrafts from the heated land, the plane began to rock again. "Is this what you call rough flying?" I asked the flight officer, Clive Limkin, as he made his way from one handhold to the next down the brown-carpeted aisle.

"Oh my word, no," he said calmly, settling into the seat next to me with the flight's paperwork. "She gets rough when we're low. On a good day we fly as low as 500 feet—because of the short legs, as we call them. For example, one run takes only four minutes, from Koolatah station to Dunbar, and another eight. At that altitude, you get a lot of hot, thin air— turbulence." He took my ticket and jotted figures on a cargo sheet. "It doesn't affect the flying badly, though."

Beneath our plane, the land had changed again. Clive looked up from his paperwork. "All this is grazing country," he told me. As far ahead as I could see, flat biscuit-colored earth reached away, gouged by dead dry riverbeds, sprinkled with green scrub. "It's what you'd call hungry land. Plants come up quickly with a rain, then go off quickly too. You're seeing the land at its best now."

It must have been Englishmen, accustomed to abundant rainfall and green countryside, who originated the persistent notion that desert covers most of Australia's interior. Certainly enough, large parts of the outback properly called semidesert look dead much of the time. Every summer, soil there gets hard, dusty—dry as a brick. And after a drought of five to ten years, even scientists, who classify a third of the continent as genuine desert, begin to think that the stricken area might be added to the death list.

But then rain comes and amazing things happen. Sharp, spiny spinifex grass springs up in clumps, and sometimes in fields growing as tall as ripe wheat. Acacia trees of many types and sizes burst to life like green fire-works. And wild flowers—thousands of varieties, some of them not yet classified — crowd so closely that it's hard to walk without stepping on a blossom. Millions of cattle munch a living from land like this.

A whine came from the open cockpit door, and I watched the lower edge of a wing ease down to break our speed. The plane aimed toward a white windsock and slowly glided to the earth runway of a town named Croydon. At the turn of the century, miners scratched fortunes in gold from the land around the town, and the settlement itself held some 6,500 people. But a few decades ago the mineral wealth gave out. Croydon's quicksilver populace moved on. Clive passed 300 pounds of cargo from the plane for the 105 citizens remaining, and we moved on too.

I imagine a stranger wandering without supplies in the land we hurtled past would die as surely as a traveler lost on the Sahara. Yet, looking beyond the rivet-studded wings, I saw nothing recalling the ferocious hostility of the great arid strip of Africa I had crossed a year before. Here, I knew, green shrubs and open forests whispered to the dry, cooling breeze. The country looked peaceful and quite inviting, provided you like space. But it remains as silent, as empty of human life as the sun-tormented wastes of Egypt.

The outback has limited settlement for two simple reasons: soil deficiencies and, more important, water scarcity. In vast areas, the earth needs phosphorus, nitrogen, or sulphur before plants can grow plentiful and nourishing enough to support more animals and people. Soil in smaller parts of the country requires applications of copper, iron, manganese, or zinc, molybdenum, boron, or cobalt. Many graziers now enrich their lands. Many do not; first their properties need a more reliable supply of water. For the country as a whole, this problem begins and ends with lack of rain. Parching under one of the most arid climate belts on earth, Australia is the driest of all the world's continents. Seventy-one percent of the land receives less precipitation than San Francisco's 20 inches or so per year. Well over half this area doesn't get 10. A few outback-dwellers feel in luck with 5 inches.

AS IMPORTANT as the coming of rain is the way it comes. A little girl from a station north of Broken Hill told a School of the Air teacher that her 4-year-old brother cried in fright when a few droplets splashed his face; he had never before seen water coming out of the air. Travelers in regions of heavy seasonal rains might well feel a similar fear when summer skies grow black with clouds and then burst in roaring thunderstorms, making shallow lakes that reach the horizon, turning empty riverbeds to crawling muddy flows many miles wide. Erratic, uncontrolled, the rain that does come goes largely to waste in runoff and evaporation.

Up where the Gulf of Carpentaria drives a shaft of sea deep into the continent, station owners have seasonal rivers to help them along. Dropping toward the next stop on its route, the plane vaulted the Norman River, a string of water holes in the dry season, but a natural cattle trough running for 260 miles when the wet season fills it to capacity.

Flowing wide and tan between ribbons of green trees, the stream I saw below sustains life of its own as well: 40-pound catfish, shovelnose sharks, giant perch, and saltwater crocodiles in from the seas of southern Asia.

The crocodiles, some weighing more than a ton, come to wage a contest with creatures of the land. Dingoes, Australia's wild dogs, know all about the war. Before they cross a river, they howl on the bank, luring reptiles from a mile or so around. Then they race upstream and paddle for their lives. Aboriginal hunters once used this lure too. They howled like dogs until yellow-green eyes peeked above the surface of the water, then hurled spears for more white tail flesh than a big man could carry.

The crocs have tricks of their own, according to north-country Australians. A 25-foot bull, with decades of experience behind him, seems to know that dogs and cattle and men live by habit. So he waits, watching his prey come for water evening after evening, at a usual time, at a favorite place. One evening he is there. A tail thrashes, jaws snap, and a creature of the land slips under the river.

Our DC-3 stirred up a little dust storm as it settled on a runway of maroon earth. With an hour or so between a change of planes, I stepped into a paradox of cooling air and blowtorch sun to find a taxi to the old goldfields port town of Normanton.

Mrs. Beryl Raisin obliged. A smiling woman in green canvas hat and white frock with a change apron tied around her waist, she drove me into town in one of her two cabs. "This place—it's shrunk a lot in the past 75 years," she explained. "Used to have a population of 6,000 in the 1880's. Now it's got about 450 in the area."

I saw perhaps ten as I strolled down a wide main street, down the middle where a strip of grass struggled to live on baked soil. A barefoot little girl hopped-skipped-and-jumped past the National Theatre, a roofless enclosure with metal walls and rough wooden benches inside. A few men chatted on the board sidewalk around an old hotel, leaning against veranda posts that were rotting away at the base. A couple of Aboriginal cowboys, called ringers or stockmen here, squatted in the shade outside a fiberboard cafe, broad-brimmed hats sheltering their eyes.

I saw no one else in the streets of Normanton. Mrs. Raisin drove me past tired wooden homes and back to the airstrip, where another DC-3 waited. As I boarded with two white-robed nuns, a child and a big rag doll, a pair of Aboriginal stockmen, and a woman carrying a caged blue parakeet, the plane hit its weight limit. Cargo took up the rest of the load.

TURNING SOUTHWARD, away from the gulf and its promise of yearly monsoonal rains, we saw the last of the open forest end abruptly in a wiggly line. Grassland lay beyond, already beige two months after the December-to-March wet season. It held not a sign of movement except for sliding cloud shadows.

I wondered where the cattle were. Through Australia, the herds add up to 18,000,000 head and make the country the world's second-ranking beef exporter, after Argentina. "You look out there for the water," one of the Aboriginal station hands told me, motioning toward the window. "You find cattle there. They usually graze not more than maybe four miles from the water. They go farther, they might perish."

Stockmen, sheepmen, and prospectors of the late 19th century swap yarns in a Queensland grog shanty, a favored meeting place for scattered outback-dwellers. Station owners seeking hands frequently hired them in such rustic pubs.

As the plane raced its own shadow across the plains, I found the water — little bright pools scattered like silver coins over the earth.

Geologically speaking, Australia was born lucky in a way. For even in its dry and withered age, it does have some reliable water, a flow that slowly seeps through porous layers of earth into artesian basins under large areas of the continent. Our flight route passed over part of the Great Artesian Basin, which underlies an arid area somewhat larger than the Republic of Mongolia. Since the first bore tapped this enormous reservoir near a town named Bourke in 1880, drillers have found five more major basins and smaller ones as well. Today, a third of the continent gets water from subterranean shafts that altogether yield 300,000,000 gallons every day, some gushing up under natural pressure, some pumped to the surface by windmills.

The bores go deep, sometimes down as far as 7,000 feet. And the liquid bursts out highly mineralized. Scientists talk about the day when sun-powered distillation plants may free the water of salts. Then, perhaps, it will irrigate great fields of wheat and other crops. For the time being, however, Australians are content that bore-water sustains most of their sheep and cattle.

Homesteads rise in this land like manicured oases, neat green squares where flowering trees and gardens crowd around buildings of wood or corrugated metal. Little more than 20 minutes out of Normanton, we banked toward the homestead of Wondoola station, a cluster of red roofs in a patch of verdure, and landed almost at the front door.

We didn't stay long. A new white car skidded up to the passenger hatch. The driver, in black sleeveless shirt and wide-brimmed hat, shouted "G'day." Our crew dragged sacks of potatoes and onions down the aisle. Aboriginal station hands lifted the load into the car trunk. "See you next week." The door slammed. We leaped into the sky.

A map of Queensland looks gray with place names, most of them marking homesteads. Crowded country, people would have called this at the turn of the century, when one man controlled a collection of holdings twice as large as England. Outback-dwellers farther west would call it crowded too. On their lean land, where a single steer may need a square mile of grazing room, simple economic necessity creates stations the size of small countries. Some Australians tour their holdings in private airplanes. Others have never fully explored the property they own. But Wondoola's next-door neighbors, on a station called Iffley, live only 11 minutes away at 145 knots air speed.

From 1,800 feet, we dropped to a grass strip. Three Aborigines met us in a utility truck and began to unload cargo. As station hands, earning a basic weekly wage of about $28 plus keep, they do anything that needs doing on the property. They ride the boundaries to keep stock from straying, spending ten hours a day in the saddle, living like explorers, sleeping in bedrolls around campfires of gidgee, mulga, or ironwood. At other times they work at branding, fencing, sinking bores, cutting tracks, driving trucks, or breaking wild horses. Gambling, fighting, and shooting kangaroos and dingoes add diversion to their days.

But then one day distant tribal rituals or memories of faraway kin call some Aboriginal hands on walkabout. "He might be your best stockman," one station owner explained, "but you never know if he'll be around from this week to the next. Out of the clear blue he'll come up to the homestead and say, 'Boss, I'm going walkabout now.' There's no keeping him. Off he goes with no more than a rifle and the clothes on his back."

In some areas, I've heard, Aborigines stroll away with spears and no clothes at all. Elsewhere, they might pool their money to buy a car and come back in an airplane.

On most stations, you'll find stockmen of European extraction too. Wheeling their horses in a cloud of orange dust, wrestling a half-ton of steer to the ground for branding, they look like men born to the land. Some were. But many of them come from cities, teen-agers chasing adventure who arrive dressed like movie cowboys, hardly able to ride a sawhorse. Most new chums, as these hands are called, go back to the cities after a couple of years. So dark-skinned Australians, some fathered by desert nomads, and white men who love the wilds and shun the cities remain the hard core of the outback work force.

Racing away from Iffley, our plane began to bounce and slide in the updrafts of a warm afternoon. Flies, which breed as thickly in the outback as mosquitoes in a swamp, paced the Plexiglas windows, wringing their wiry hands as they grew sluggish in the cool cabin air. I shooed the glass clear and watched the horizon, a smooth and perfect circle now, the land dead flat and tan. It was like flying over a pancake.

Just as Australians adapted the country as best they could for cattle, clearing trees and drilling deep for water, so have they adapted cattle for the country. The earliest settlers stopped at Africa's Cape of Good Hope and picked up zebu stock. This breed and small Bengal cattle brought from India in 1791 gave inferior meat and little milk. So graziers imported European stock. Pastoralists noticed that Asian animals could graze farther from water, maintaining more weight in dry spells. They also endured the heat better than European beasts. In recent decades, cattle from East and West were crossbred, producing stock both profitable and drought-resistant.

"We got drought-resistant everything back here," a stockman told me once, "grass, scrub, people — you name it. Me mate, he says he's working on a drought-resistant pig now," the man smiled, "crossing Berkshire sows with artesian bores."

PERHAPS TO GUIDE aircraft over country without features, Canobie station shouted its name to the sky in huge white letters painted on a rooftop. We circled, as the law requires, to be sure the strip was clear. Then we glided down, past refuse heaps of cans and bottles, over slivers of evaporating floodwater, beyond more than a dozen buildings in a tight square, onto the grass landing field. The pilot handed a few boxes of vegetables and six cans of beer to a man in white shirt and glasses. The man waved and drove away in a yellow car. Props raced, wing flaps wiggled in a test, and we hopped off from the final station on our route.

Forty-three minutes southwest, I left the DC-3 at an industrial oasis called Mount Isa. An oasis indeed, the town lies 500 miles from the populous cities of the east coast and very much alone in the dusty red outback. A seemingly limitless mineral lode supports its 17,000 people, holding silver, lead, zinc, and one of the most important copper deposits in the world. How well supported they are I saw aboard another plane bound north for the tropical city of Darwin. Climbing clear of scrubby hills, we caught a startling glimpse of an enormous man-made lake named Moondara, where speedboats cut a spiderweb of wakes in the heat of a semidesert evening.

At 16,000 feet we chased an orange seam where night was meeting day until the sun blazed gloriously into its desert grave. Left in the ponderous void of the outback, we could only wonder what might lie in the ocean of black below our swift, warm room.

A cattle drive, perhaps — the night rider singing to soothe a nervous herd, while drover, stockmen, horse tailer, and cook sit around a fire placing bets on the time a satellite will cross the sky. How long would they roam from one water hole to the next? I've heard of cattle drives that crept over the country for two years.

Certainly road trains roared through the darkness. Gargantuan trucks powered by diesel engines with 22 gears, they do the work of drovers at somewhat greater cost when station owners want to move their stock to market quickly. With five trailers as large as furniture vans, each train can carry a hundred head.

For a time, we followed the 403-mile Barkly Highway that leads the road trains westward from Mount Isa. The pavement runs out of Queensland into the huge, virtually vacant block of land called the Northern Territory. In the middle of the Territory, halfway across the continent, the route meets the Stuart Highway, the only other paved road of any size in Australia's heartland. That strip of bitumen, 20 feet wide and 954 miles long, provides Darwin's single land link with the rest of the country, running south to the town of Alice Springs at the continental center.

Our flight veered away from the Barkly, aiming northwest over country where only bush tracks go. No towns twinkled along the nonstop route. In all the Northern Territory's sprawl—as large as France, Spain, and Italy combined—Alice Springs and Darwin remain the only sizable settlements. Nor did we sight the lonely lights of homesteads. The region holds barely 60,000 citizens, leaving great stretches of country devoid of human habitation. Beef cattle graze where rainfall allows, giving the Territory its major industry. But even on productive semidesert, man and his half-wild domestic stock live amid raw nature.

Where tracks and roads slash through the country, drivers stay alert for kangaroos, especially at night when a 150-pounder might plop down into headlight beams at the end of a 25-foot bound.

Termite mounds rise by the thousand, insect cities of hard mud reaching 20 feet in height. Each one crawls with as many as 3,000,000 inhabitants—a king and an egg-laying queen, soldiers patrolling a maze of corridors, workers stacking quarter-inch lengths of grass as neatly as firewood in their food chambers.

NEAR THE NORTHERN COAST, monsoonal rains blowing in from the Arafura Sea turn miles of lagoon-dotted earth to verdant swamp. That's buffalo country. The native Indian cattle, imported from Asia to provide meat for early settlers, now run wild 100,000 strong.

Just south of Darwin, we saw flames cutting neat lines in the black infinity of emptiness. I imagined Aborigines streaked and spotted with white paint, wearing feathers glued to the skin with human blood, dancing in the celebration, secular or sacred, called corroboree. For this is their country, too, a place of many church missions and government settlements for the black Australians. They dance and hunt in the wilds of Arnhem Land, I knew. And on Melville Island, just offshore from Darwin, their customs rule the mode of life as much as white men's ways. Pointing out the dots and bars of flame, I asked the pilot, "Campfires?"

But no, we still flew very high and the flames were larger than they looked. "Bushfires," he answered.

"Namargan," the Aborigines might explain, the legendary lightning man filling the night with fiery rage.

Essential repair near Normanton: Thousands of windmills, some with vanes as long as 15 feet, pump water from basins underlying a third of the continent.

NATIONAL GEOGRAPHIC PHOTOGRAPHER WINFIELD PARKS

NATIONAL GEOGRAPHIC PHOTOGRAPHER WINFIELD PARKS

Homestead buildings on Wrotham Park cattle station cluster among scrub gums between a muddy reservoir and a dry creek. Planes from Cairns, 125 miles away on Queensland's east coast, land mail and supplies every week on the earth airstrip. Three times the size of Rhode Island, the 2.5-million-acre station—like many of Australia's larger holdings —has its own small plane for checking on herds. A "jackaroo," or apprentice stockman, brings in wayward bulls (opposite), and rests his horse beside the corral (right). Adventure-hunting city teen-agers join regular hands and Aboriginal stockmen in mustering, branding, and droving during ten-hour days in the saddle. More than a third of the nation's 18,000,000 cattle graze Queensland stations.

131

Merciless sun beats down on iron roofs and russet earth in Normanton. In 105-degree heat, life barely stirs at the center of the mile-long town south of the Gulf of Carpentaria. Most of the 450 inhabitants keep to the shade of deep-porched stores or stay inside houses surrounded by fenced yards of patchy grass and carefully tended trees. Thirsty beer drinkers (opposite) fight the heat at one of the town's three bars. Cooling rain comes in erratic torrents; cisterns, empty eight months of the year, catch runoff from house eaves and the council hall (center). Horses nibble grass in front of the hall, built in 1890 during the rush to goldfields farther inland. With mines long worked out, income depends on supplying cattle stations and shipping beef to market. Motor vehicles and weekly plane service ease the isolation for people living 50 miles or more from towns much like Normanton. Radio, outdoor movies, and crocodile shooting in the brackish Norman River and the Gulf of Carpentaria take up the slack of long scorching months.

NATIONAL GEOGRAPHIC PHOTOGRAPHER WINFIELD PARKS

SHIRE   COUNCI

132

NATIONAL GEOGRAPHIC PHOTOGRAPHER WINFIELD PARKS

Monument to mineral treasures, the striped smokestack of Mount Isa's copper smelter stands 503 feet high beside low, eroded hills of the Selwyn Range. Here a sprawling industrial complex taps one of Australia's richest deposits of lead, copper, zinc, and silver. A prospector found the lode in 1923 while tracking a packhorse that had slipped its hobbles. Most of the town's 17,000 people live in air-conditioned houses. Planes and trains bring beer, milk, and fruit from cities as distant as 2,000 miles. "New Australians," or immigrants, from 50 countries make up nearly one-third of the work force. At the Saturday horse race, avid fans study the handicaps; bookmakers (left) wait to take bets.

TOR EIGELAND, BLACK STAR

Termites' high-rise apartment houses, decades old, tower twice as tall as six-footer David Bridge of the National Geographic staff. South of Darwin, thousands of such mud structures up to 20 feet high built by Naustitermes triodiae *stand like petrified tree stumps amid tropical eucalypts. Josephine Tan of Singapore (above) gazes at a slab-shaped nest raised by* Amitermes meridionalis; *below, she examines the broad face of a similar one.* Meridionalis *mounds always point north and south like compass needles, earning them the name of "magnetic nests." Areas with numbers of such slabs resemble cemeteries. As temperature and humidity change, millions of the tiny, blind insects move back and forth between tunnels underground and cells in the mound walls. In some cubicles, they store finely cut grass for food—in others, dead companions.* 137

Bull water buffalo soaks in a water hole on Goodparla station, southeast of Darwin. About 100,000 buffalo roam wild over seasonally swampy coastal areas of the Northern Territory, descendants of stock imported from Asia in the 1800's. For decades, hunters have shot the animals for their hides. Cattlemen now catch and domesticate the buffalo, breeding them for "buff steak" and hamburger. At Goodparla, stockmen in a jeep (top right) drive a bull back to the herd; mounted Aborigines quietly prod animals away from a cool mud wallow toward greener fenced pastures. Stockmen (below) stop in a clear stream to dip up drinking water.

In the glare of tropical sunrise, Tiwi tribesmen in Snake Bay, Melville Island, spear and bag fish swept into a weir by ebbing tide. In deeper water a spear-fisherman poises for a thrust from a dugout canoe. About 1,150 Aborigines live in villages and government settlements on Melville and neighboring Bathurst Island, off the north-central coast of Australia. Below, at a corroboree—a series of dances and songs lasting for hours—Tiwi pantomime buffalo as an old man sings. Raised arms mimic horns.

White-haired woodcarver files smooth a stylized buffalo near frame houses of Melville Island's Snake Bay community, one of 14 Aboriginal settlements directed by the Northern Territory administration. The Tiwi craftsman touches up the work of a year for sale in Darwin, 70 miles away. Until the early 1900's naked Tiwi armed with sharpened sticks lived by killing game for household camps; women gathered roots, nuts, worms, and larvae for food. Today the child watching the carver, and the intent young artist (left), learn new ways that the government hopes will equip them to share in Australia's expanding prosperity. At the settlement school, teacher Happy Cook encourages a class learning to speak, read, and write English. Few of Australia's 100,000 Aborigines remain nomads dependent on spear, woomera, and boomerang.

7

The West: Mountains Of Iron, Islands of Oil

BRUCE BRANDER

WHEN YOU WAKE UP under a lazy ceiling fan in Darwin, you're closer to the Equator than Bangkok or Tahiti, Kingston or Khartoum. In the Wet, as Australians call the tropical rainy season, a monsoonal storm may rouse you, rain roaring like a locomotive on the corrugated metal roof. In the Dry, you'll open louvered sun-shutters to crisp blue sky, light as hard and dazzling as polished brass, breezes in the 80's brushing palms with the scent of frangipani.

Arriving when the climate in the middle of Australia's northern coast was at its balmy best, I woke up on a cot in the corner of a guesthouse veranda. The hotels were jammed, mostly with vacationists from chilly southern cities. The veranda too had been jammed a day earlier, with stockmen who had come to town to celebrate Anzac Day.

In one way or another, everybody down under commemorates the 25th of April, 1915, when the Australian and New Zealand Army Corps landed on Gallipoli Peninsula in Turkey. They fought "Johnnie Turk," as they called the enemy, to a stalemate, enduring eight months of bitter fighting, sickness, rain, heat, and winter gales. By the end of the campaign, the tall tanned people from below the Equator had established an international legend for heroic tenacity.

In big cities, veterans of that battle and a great many since march behind brass bands. In the smallest country towns, they gather at dawn—

Features molded by a harsh land, Western Australian Harry Jacoby reflects the determination of a people to develop their country's wealth. His state, nearly a million square miles in area, occupies a third of the continent. Immense mineral and agricultural resources spur a new, carefully planned prosperity there.

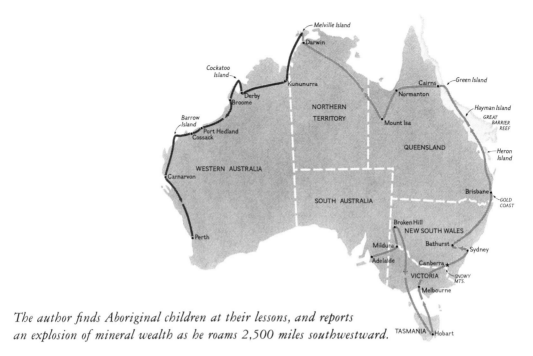

The author finds Aboriginal children at their lessons, and reports
an explosion of mineral wealth as he roams 2,500 miles southwestward.

perhaps only a dozen or so—medals jingling on lapels as they pray at a
memorial service. In Darwin, the stockmen had prayed and marched, and
then set out on a week-long spree. "I blew months in wages," said my
veranda roommate, who had stayed behind to get rid of his barcoo rot—a
skin ailment hard to cure under conditions in the wilds. "It was just
grand," he grinned, flicking on a transistor radio and searching under his
cot for a half-gallon flagon of beer.

Shortly after sunrise, Northern Territory Welfare Director Harry
Giese drove me to the airport. Tall, slender, and always talking exuberantly
about his work, he supervises 28 Aboriginal communities that speckle
more than half a million square miles of terrain. Today he had in mind a
routine visit to the Tiwi tribesmen of Melville Island. A spare seat in his
chartered plane was mine. Twin propellers dissolved to whizzing pools
and we lifted off Darwin's flat peninsula, then skimmed over fat fingers of
sand and mangrove swamp that pointed seaward.

When Captain Cook dropped anchor far to the southeast in Botany
Bay, some 200,000 Stone Age nomads foraged over the continent, hundreds of loosely organized tribes, each claiming a territory of its own.
Where they came from no one knows for certain. Most anthropologists
class the dark-skinned wanderers as a separate race named Australoid
and believe the group migrated from Asia at least 100 centuries ago.

They adapted to the worn and weary land superbly. They hunted
kangaroo and emu, dug the earth for roots and grubs, and thrived where
less resourceful peoples could not hope to survive.

Then, 18 years after Captain Cook arrived, European settlers began to
upset the delicate balance between man and hunting land. Sporadically,
Aborigines resisted the agricultural invaders. More often, they went to
work for them, settling in rustic camps on the outskirts of towns and
homestead plots.

But dependence brought cultural and personal deterioration. The

Aboriginal population dropped to about 70,000 by the turn of the present century. As recently as 1939, some authorities believed the race would die out altogether. Then the group began to grow again. Today dependence of a different sort — on medical care, food, and shelter offered at government settlements and church missions — assures healthy survival of 100,000 dark-skinned Australians.

Survival and far more lies ahead for Aborigines. Across the 16-mile width of Clarence Strait, Harry Giese began to point out changes in their ancient way of living. We flew over eucalyptus forest, a blanket of woolly treetops that spreads over most of Melville Island's 2,925 square miles. But near the airstrip, built for fighter planes during World War II, we saw a thousand acres of cultivated cypress. Islanders learn forestry, Giese said, getting cash income and job training at the same time.

A National Geographic Society Expedition that came to Melville Island in 1954 found vestiges of Tiwi material culture as primitive as that of all mankind 50,000 years ago. Tribesmen hunted wallabies and bandicoots, caught rats and pythons, dug for lizards and collected the tender hearts of cabbage palms. They stripped the woody shells of stringybark trees to make simple lean-to shelters. They chanted the fish's song, stamped the shark dance, and surrounded their graves with carved and painted tree trunks that rose twice as tall as the artisans themselves.

Driving to the government village on an inlet called Snake Bay, we found Tiwi women sewing infants' clothing, tribal hunters preparing meals in a large communal dining hall, and children reciting English lessons at a two-room school.

"They still maintain much of their culture," Giese said as we walked past scattered wooden dwellings built on short stilts and painted in gentle pastel colors. Women in cotton dresses and some in skirts alone looked up from outdoor fireplaces and waved as they cooked fish caught the night before, or swept the dusty ground outside their homes with twiggy brooms. "They hunt on weekends," he continued. "And they're perfectly free to leave the settlement if they want to go back to the bush for awhile. But when they're here receiving food and lodging, we try to teach them to work as white Australians do. The long-term goal here is to have a community which is entirely self-sufficient."

TOTAL INTEGRATION is the still more distant goal throughout the nation. Affirming the feasibility of this plan, some members of the race already live within their land's new culture. Aborigines have served their country in South Viet Nam. Others work as government officials. Dark-skinned sportsmen have won national and international championships. And two Aborigines have received university degrees in recent years.

Some have taken jobs in Darwin, a place that reminded me of a holiday town. Businessmen go about their work in shorts and open-neck shirts. Women in sunhats and cool, casual frocks stroll among shops. Most people wear sandals, or no footwear at all. And if it gets too hot, offices may close so citizens can retreat to breezy homes on stilts.

Old-timers around town remember days when Darwin looked more like the setting of a tropical adventure tale. Ever since 1869, when South Australians planted the settlement on its deep harbor, Darwin had drawn its people from the world over.

From Malaya and Japan, pearl divers came to harvest local waters. Chinese laborers arrived to work on a railway lancing 146 miles southeast toward gold strikes of the 1870's. And miners came to town, flooding in by ship, coming up from diggings to the south through the last two decades of the 19th century. Brown fishermen sailed down from the island of New Guinea. And seamen of every color and nation jumped ship to stay in the land where promise seemed as big as the horizon.

The hard-drinking shanty town with its exotic population sweltered through the decades until World War II. Then, with the fall of Singapore, Japanese forces moved south through Asia, and warplanes hailed bombs on Darwin. A new breed of strangers poured in—some 100,000 Australian and American soldiers posted in the Northern Territory to guard against full-scale attack.

But Japanese troops never crossed the Arafura Sea. Darwin rose again, this time as a bright and modern city with more reason for existence than it ever had before. Attempts to develop the Territory—its minerals and agricultural potential—brought civil servants up from the south. Now they make up nearly a third of the 24,500 citizens. Another reason for the city's growth lies in its proximity to Asia. Closer to Singapore than to Sydney, the port serves as a customs station and fueling stop for jet traffic with the Near North.

Yet you still see every race amid the futuristic banks and administration buildings, people ranging in color from ebony to olive, from honey-toned to Saxon pink. In impeccably modern hotels, you'll still find pearl divers and prospectors chatting over frosted beer glasses. And you may well hear a yarn about crocodile shooting, a wild-buffalo safari, or a ritual murder among the Aborigines. Darwin, after all, remains an outpost. Where city streets end, the whole Australian wilderness begins.

DRIVING NOT FAR EAST of Darwin to a land of great lagoons, you feel you've gone back to the day when earthly life came into being. Leave the car on a bush track near one of the swampy pools and walk to the water's edge. Warm, stagnant, perhaps a mile across, the lagoon and its environs teem with life. You might find a tree python writhing overhead, or a four-foot monitor lizard rooted still as a statue on the shore, hissing at your approach, lashing out a long purple forked tongue.

Certainly you'll find birds—thousands of them. Australian cranes, called brolgas, stride in pairs along the shore like old men in gray suits rapt in thoughtful conversation. An armada of pelicans glides by in perfect formation, all dipping baggy bills at once for fish, breaking ranks only when they thrash the water and rise into the sky like seaplanes. Creep silently through pandanus thickets and you'll spot herons, ibis, and darters, red-tailed cockatoos, and ducks. Egrets descend in numbers so enormous they look like a blizzard. Magpie geese, jet black with a wide white stripe over breast and back, outnumber them.

Camels imported from India take supplies into Western Australia's interior in the late 19th century. The pack animals, ideally suited to the dry, cruel climate, numbered some 4,000 in 1900 and bore most of the state's overland freight. Trucks and railroads replaced the last of the caravans in the 1930's. Today, some camels roam wild; others carry the gear of prospectors.

RICHARD SCHLECHT

The geese usually feed in the shallows, poking around marsh plants for succulent bulbs in the liquid mud below. During the Wet, they peck at ripening wild rice. In the late 1950's, they found one feeding ground suddenly enriched. At an area called Humpty Doo, some 40 miles southeast of Darwin, an American firm began to plant a commercial rice crop, with several thousand acres of the grain planned for the Asian export market. The geese flapped down in honking flocks to devour the planting. Scarecrows went up, to no avail. Noisemakers rattled and spotlights swept the fields, but that too failed to keep the birds away. Poison killed some of the marauders, but other birds replaced them. Eventually, farmers called in the army. Soldiers set up machine guns, harassing the geese with clattering bursts of fire. The birds, undaunted, settled out of range and ate their fill. Though farmers packed up and abandoned the land, research has shown that careful controls over land-selection, planting, and watering could beat the geese and save the rice.

A short, hard rain had replenished the lagoons the night before I left. In a big twin-engine plane bound southwest for the city of Perth, I soared into sky washed and polished like a lens. The aerial hop I meant to take was a big one; we could plan on nearly eight hours aboard. Yet in the whole 1,685-mile span of land we crossed, we would touch not a single community of more than township size.

"This country—it looks like nothing, right?" my seatmate remarked as we shot out of the Northern Territory into the State of Western Australia. As politely as I could, I agreed. Tidal flats and sun-baked scrub lay below. Southward a tremendous wrinkled wasteland stretched away, dry valleys that Australians call rivers streaking between hot knuckles of rock.

149

I knew enormous deserts reached almost to the southern coast 1,150 miles away—the Great Sandy Desert, the Gibson, the Great Victoria. Largest of all Australian states, with more than four times the area of Texas, Western Australia can look very much indeed like nothing. "But don't let it fool you," the man asserted with the proprietary pride that all the nation's people feel about the particular state they call home. "This place—why, it's full of loot."

And loot I found, in developments new and booming, so fascinating from the start that I left the flight, then roamed around the state for many days to come.

The far-north town of Kununurra looked for all the world like a modern Sydney suburb parachuted into a field of ten-foot cane grass. The community of 930 people rushed into existence in 1963, when the state and Commonwealth governments finished a diversion dam across the fast-flowing Ord River. With abundant water trapped for irrigation, pioneering farmers began to cover 30,000 acres of rich, black alluvial soil with American-bred Rex and Deltapine cotton. To the independent growers, the Ord River Irrigation Scheme provides a way to prosperous living. To Australia, it's a hopeful experiment, a foothold in hot, seasonally wet, unsettled land where millions of riverside acres offer rich agricultural potential.

CARAVANS OF CAMELS imported from Asian lands crossed the wilds of the state within living memory. Now the dromedaries run free, and maps designed for travelers say "horse track" and "stock route" and "4-wheel-drive only." Following the sparse succession of dotted lines across cattle stations the size of medieval kingdoms, you can pick a path through rough rock hills all the way to the Indian Ocean.

But most travelers out of Kununurra take a longer, safer drive on a beef road. The dusty route leads south, then west, past miles of station country to the cattle shipping port of Derby on the northwest coast.

Leaving Derby by ship, as I did, you might witness—literally—an explosion of wealth. Every morning at ten o'clock, and again at 5 p.m., mining crews on Cockatoo Island 83 miles from the port blast free another avalanche of ironstone. Trucks move in. They load the broken earth and groan away to crushers. Sixty to 70 percent of the rust-red earth is pure iron. And the cliff-ringed island, almost four miles long, is made of high-grade ore from end to end, a reserve estimated at 15,000,000 tons. A few minutes by small plane across the water, bare-chested drilling and blasting crews hack at another 45,000,000 tons on Koolan Island.

At 19 knots, our ship slid southward on a purple-blue sea, only a slight rise and fall hinting of the ground swell. The Indian Ocean as far as we could see wore the sheen of heavy oil, disturbed only when a school of dolphin stirred up a patch of whitecaps, or silvery flying fish glided a hundred feet or so and scraped a herringbone trail before they vanished.

Most coastal ships that run between Darwin and Perth put into the little northwest port of Broome with cargo for its 3,200 citizens. But traffic from the sea runs far lighter today than a few generations ago, when luggers manned with Asian crews set sail to reap a rich harvest of pearl shell. The industry, never very stable anywhere, declined sharply after World War II. Plastics nearly filled the world's need for buttons. But the multiracial town of Broome remains, shipping fish and beef south, sending live oysters north to pearl farms at Kuri Bay and Cape Leveque.

Tides slipping out from northwest ports often leave ships standing high and dry on smooth tan mud. The water level falls as much as 40 feet. As the ocean surges, engineers begin to think of dams and generators crackling out a bonanza of electric power. Frenchmen who helped to build the world's first tidal power station, on the English Channel near St. Malo, came to Australia in the early 1960's to inspect this segment of the coast. With its many sounds and deep bays, the region offers, they affirmed, "the best conditions for tidal power in the world."

Until recent years, no one appreciated Australia's western shoreline very much. Its 17th-century discoverers, sailing out from Holland by way of Africa's southern tip, combed the coast for signs of gold or spice or other riches worth their notice. They found only bleak land and the naked Aborigine. For later voyagers bent on prosperous trade, the continent had value only as a landmark; it told them when to change course northward for the Spice Islands of Indonesia.

More than three centuries later, the captain of the ship I sailed on looked back on his decade of coastal trading. "This place was dead when I started on the run," he recalled. "We hardly saw any ships — not even many sea birds. All the ports were dead." And then he added, "If anybody had told me a few years ago about what's happening now, I wouldn't have believed it."

Port Hedland, 370 miles south of Broome, shows the story he went on to tell. Big floating dredges inhaled silt to make the harbor deeper, then dumped it out to make new land. A new jetty stabbed out 600 feet. Pipes, drilling apparatus, and silvery railway tracks lay in piles just off the main streets of the town. Engineers, geologists, surveyors, and laborers packed the pubs to fight the heat with beer at 50 cents a bottle. Hotels scarcely held their guests in crowded rooms and cots on the verandas.

A new lode of hematite, averaging 65 percent iron, lies 70 miles inland at a place called Mount Goldsworthy. Four hundred feet thick, 2,200 feet long, the known reserve of some 41,000,000 tons will rumble over rail tracks to the port revived to ship it.

The tale of new mineral wealth continues 150 miles down the coast at the brand-new port of Dampier. Ride an empty ore train 175 miles into the Hamersley Ranges and you'll find a whole mountain of high-grade iron ore at the end of the line. Discovered in 1962, Mount Tom Price promises a reserve of 500,000,000 tons.

Men knew long ago that Western Australia held useful minerals in its dry wasteland. But they didn't know how much; perhaps enough for the country's future, the Commonwealth government hoped. An embargo kept iron ore from exportation — and from full exploitation due to lack of funds at home. New discoveries increased, holding a promise of enormous wealth, and the government, in 1960, modified the embargo. Development funds poured in from America, Britain, Japan. That spurred more exploration. A radio I carried as I traveled through the state summed up the results of the past two years: an average of one major mineral discovery every month, most of them in Western Australia.

Land that once seemed largely null and void offers manganese and copper, tin, bauxite, lead, and gold. A nickel discovery at a place called Kambalda appears to be one of the richest deposits on earth. But new-found iron leads by far in national importance. Australia now ranks among the world's most bountiful sources of the ore.

Rolling south in a cockeye bob, as Western Australians call their local gales, our ship passed yet another recent strike of riches. Barrow Island, 18 miles long and less than half that wide, gushed up oil in 1964. A small matter, a couple of dozen wells might seem, compared to massive iron lodes. But greater than the strike itself was its hint of further promise. Australia needs oil of its own more than any other major mineral vital to the modern age. For years, petroleum has been the costliest single item on its import list. Strikes at Barrow gave new hope to international prospecting efforts. A few days after we sailed by, another gusher—this one on Pasco Island two miles to the south—offered still more encouragement to prospectors in the wilds of Western Australia.

Investment of big money looks riskier than usual in undeveloped country. So the state seemed unusually pleased when the United States Navy came to the Exmouth Gulf, halfway down the lonely coast, with $70,000,000 in U. S. funds for a new communications base. Using antennas that soar higher than the Eiffel Tower, very low frequency transmitters at the station keep contact with both surface ships and submarines. For the state, one expert on the region testified, "the job could set the pattern for big capital investment in other parts of the north. . . ."

PROBES into the heavens brought still more capital to the town of Carnarvon, 560 sea miles north of Perth. A tracking station operated by Australians to aid the United States space program began to function near the region's banana plantations and vegetable farms in 1964. Maintained at a cost of a million dollars a year, the installation adds data to information from a worldwide chain of tracking stations.

Growth has come before to Western Australia, creating boomtowns as it surged, leaving ghost towns as it ebbed. But the growth today, the state believes, is here to stay.

"It's the biggest thing that's happened in all Australia since the 1850's gold rush," one mining engineer asserted. Every lode of minerals needs a brand-new town, with shopping center, swimming pool, railway, and a port that grows at the same pace. And every town needs population, irrigated farms, and permanent supplies of water.

"That's what's happening now," he continued. "But come back in another ten years and see what it looks like. Opening up this state amounts to putting the second half of the country in gear, my word it does!"

Churning up dust from an ironstone cliff, a driller sinks a blast hole to a depth of 40 feet on Cockatoo Island, near the coast of northwestern Australia.

Blasting obscures the terraces of an open-cut mine on Cockatoo Island, one of Australia's important sources of iron though less than four miles long. Twenty million tons of the mineral lie in hills and cliffs that rise nearly 400 feet from the sea. The huge electric shovel can scoop up 12 tons at a bite. Cockatoo and neighboring Koolan Island annually produce three million tons of high-grade ore for furnaces in eastern Australia. The miner at left lives and works on Cockatoo. Down the mainland coast, at Dampier, a giant carrier takes on ore from the interior to supply smelting plants in Japan, some 3,600 nautical miles away.

155

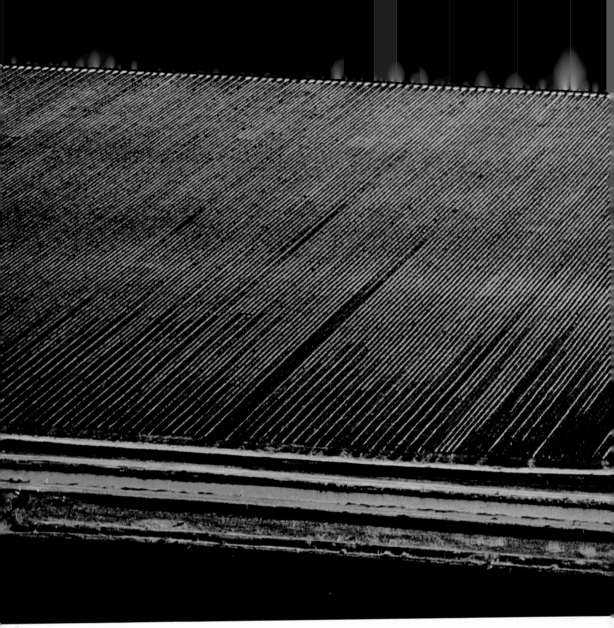

Ord River water soaks a cotton field in Western Australia's Ivanhoe Valley, part of an irrigation

Ore samples packed with minerals cover a table near Peter Costeo, who pries open a water-storage barrel. Costeo, a Perth builder-turned-prospector, struck it rich on a stake of 300 acres near Kununurra. The ore, dynamited from just below the surface, contains silver, lead, copper, gold, antimony, and zinc. On his claim, Costeo has unearthed what he calls his "museum piece," a two-ton chunk of composite ore containing mostly silver. Teatime: Costeo (on bench) shares a "cuppa" with a visitor.

TOR EIGELAND, BLACK STAR

project that ultimately may cover 200,000 acres. Farmers also plant test plots of sugar cane and grain.

"*C is for Chick . . . S is for Shoe*" *chant alphabet learners at the state school in Broome, Western Australia's old "Port of Pearls." Many of the youngsters descend from the town's polyglot population of the early 1900's — pearl divers and deckhands from Japan and Malaya, Chinese pearl buyers and European merchants, and a smattering of Filipinos and Aborigines. Established in 1883, Broome's pearling and pearl-shell industry reached its zenith around 1912, but declined when the market fell off during the world depression of the 1930's. Down from a peak of 5,500 residents to some 3,200, the town now supplies live oysters for a cultured-pearl industry 300 miles north in Kuri Bay. Pearls grown there by Australian and Japanese experts command high prices in New York, London, and Paris. Teen-agers (opposite) enjoy an impromptu basketball game on the school court. Her skirt ballooning, a barefoot pupil at St. Mary's Convent School balances on a chain-link fence. The first-grader above totals bricks numbered to help her learn math.*

Construction crew places reinforcing steel for a 600-foot concrete jetty at Port Hedland, booming northwest-coast mining port. Tugboats nudge an empty iron-ore carrier toward a nearby pier. To deepen the harbor entrance for large vessels, dredges have pumped up more than 15 million cubic yards of silt; previously, a sandbar blocked all but shallow-draft ships. Iron ore from the hinterland reaches Port Hedland by rail from Mount Goldsworthy, 70 miles to the east. In 1969 another railway will begin bringing iron ore from Mount Newman, 265 miles south. Reserves of manganese, copper, asbestos, and gold lie near the coast. Above, a hard-hatted construction worker quenches his thirst at a wharfside water bag; in the evening, life centers on the local pub.

161

In a wilderness of spinifex clumps, a drilling rig probes for oil and natural gas on Barrow Island off the northwest corner of Australia. Untouched for centuries, even by Aborigines, the desolate isle shipped its first commercial oil in 1967. The technician above operates a rig drilling 7,000 feet deep; crewmen below adjust valves on a storage tank before piping oil to a ship waiting offshore.

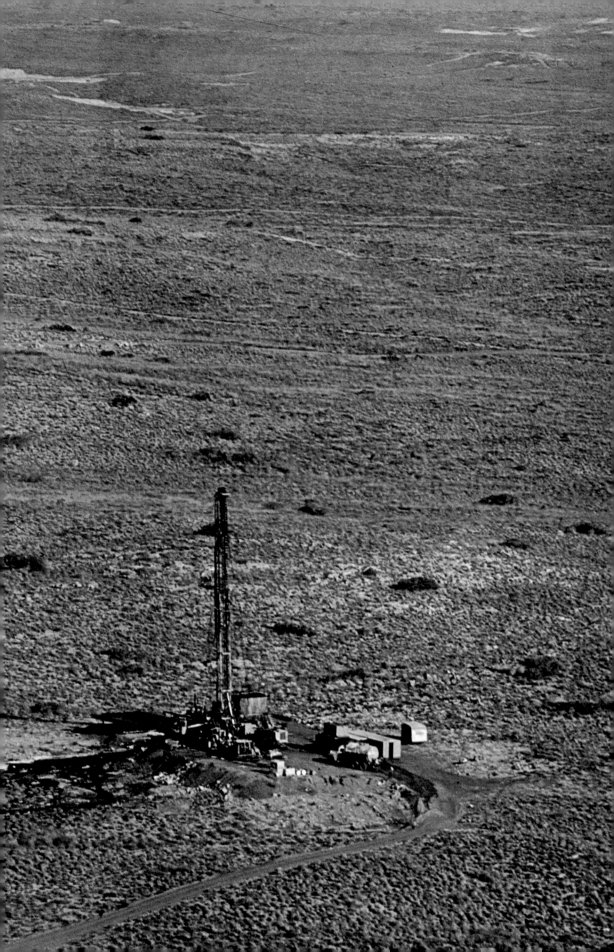

Abandoned to sand and scrub, the courthouse in the ghost town of Cossack stands on a street that throbbed with life before the turn of the century. Home then to hundreds of Asian pearl divers, Cossack began crumbling into ruin with the depletion of its pearl beds and the shifting of the industry to Broome, 480 miles to the northeast. In a poinciana tree outside the courthouse, rose-breasted galahs perch on limbs they picked bare of leaves. A young visitor walks beside the rusted railings of a neglected graveyard; seashells gathered on neighboring beaches decorate the plots.

Dish antenna 30 feet in diameter stands poised at the Carnarvon tracking station to pick up a spacecraft appearing over the horizon. Holding a "press to talk" switch, a console operator (above) gives instructions for locking on to the orbiting vehicle. Engineers stand near the cone that receives radio signals collected by the saucer and reflected from the small disk overhead. The United States and Australia developed the station as a link in the U. S. Apollo moon program.

8

Perth, Glints of Gold, And a Treeless Plain

BRUCE BRANDER

THESE DAYS you might bump into anybody on the streets of Perth. Prospectors with geology degrees, bound for treasure hunts in the northern wilderness, pass through an international airport where jets are soaring in from London and Johannesburg, Bombay and Singapore. Financiers from Melbourne and Los Angeles with boomtowns on their minds stroll into streamlined office buildings on the tree-lined business avenue called St. George's Terrace.

By the thousand, immigrants born in southern and central Europe come to labor in the outback, young men gone to the western part of Australia where people speak mostly in future tense. Japanese businessmen check into hotels so new they smell of fresh plaster, hoping to feed their ravenous steel mills with enough Australian ore to meet, in time, a third of Japan's standing requirements.

Such significance burst suddenly on Western Australia's calm and charming capital. Huddled with its port of Fremantle on the southern Indian Ocean, Perth lived its first 131 years far from the focus of Australian affairs. Sydney lies more distant than Moscow is from London. Only a lonely, rather hazardous road and a single set of train tracks link Perth with its nearest metropolitan neighbor, Adelaide, crossing 1,700 miles of virtually uninhabited plains to do it. The city grew up speaking of its eastern compatriots as "t'other-siders." Older citizens remember

Denver City Hotel in Coolgardie, Western Australia — a sturdy survivor of the gold rush of the 1890's — mirrors the American West of a century ago. During the height of the boom, the town held 24 times today's population of 500. One early resident: a young mining engineer named Herbert Hoover.

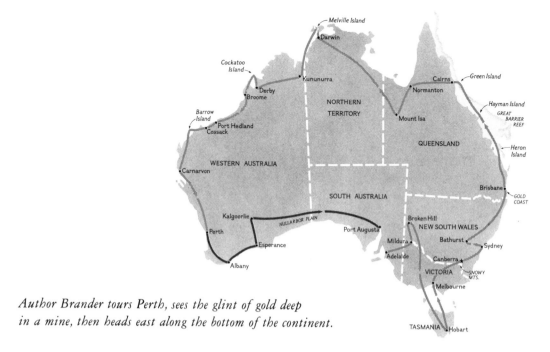

Author Brander tours Perth, sees the glint of gold deep in a mine, then heads east along the bottom of the continent.

when their state, covering one-third of the continent, wanted to secede and have a go at living entirely on its own. And younger ones still talk of decades when the region felt starved for development funds.

The change came in 1960, when the Commonwealth government modified the embargo on iron-ore exports. The mineral boom that followed has sparked growth in every direction. "We're pleased, of course," Andrew Millen, manager of the state tourist bureau, told me. "But we shan't forget that growth is for people, rather than the other way round." Calling for a car and a driver, he sent me out to see what he meant.

Growth along the ocean shore, where waves around 70° F. arched their backs and dove at sandy beaches, seemed mostly in the hands of the people. For miles, new homes of brick and wood in a great variety of architectural styles sprinkled low, scrubby sandhills.

Driving 14 miles south of Fremantle to the coastal town of Kwinana, we found new industry serving people better than usual by keeping its billows of white and yellow smoke far from the city center. An oil refinery operates here, with steelworks, an aluminum plant, a cement factory, and a fertilizer company. Large tracts of grassy hills wait for more industrial growth, adding the guarantee that Perth will keep its pure air, white buildings, and clean midtown Swan River.

The river, named after graceful red-billed black swans that have always skimmed its surface, spreads as wide as a lake for much of the 12 miles between Perth's center and the sea. Luxurious new homes spring up in view of the water. But the banks, blanketed with lawn, remain a province for picnic sites and sports grounds. And the river itself is for pleasure boats rather than for waste and commercial traffic.

Like most Australian cities, with a chance to plan while it grew, Perth set aside miles of ground for parkland. Within strolling distance from the business district, a thousand acres preserve the region's native trees, shrubs, and wild flowers. On other public lands, the snowless winters,

Mediterranean summers, and an average eight hours' sunshine a day let hibiscus bloom with English flowers under palms, the trees of Europe, and Norfolk Island pines.

Timber soars nearly 300 feet in the rain-washed southwest corner of Australia, hardwood so durable that foresters fell trees with explosives. Motoring some 250 miles south of Perth, one passes apple orchards, dairy country, and rich green sheepland to reach the tall commercial stands of eucalypts. Moving on beyond the cool caverns of karri, jarrah, and tingle trees, I stopped in the far-south port of Albany, where men add giants of the sea to the state's harvest.

"We get more than 600 sperm whales a year," Jock Murray told me. I had driven several miles past the town to find him, onto a tongue of land pointing toward the ocean, where gray rock outcrops and low scrub bring the Scottish Highlands to mind. First I looked in at the factory he manages, the Cheynes Beach Whaling Company Proprietary Ltd.

Workers had just finished cutting up whales caught the day before. With winches and cables, they had hauled the creatures from the water to a wide wooden deck. Peeling off the blubber much as one would skin a banana, they had dropped it through holes in the deck into eight-foot-wide pressure-cookers that seethed in factory rooms below. Of three whales, all more than 35 feet long, nothing remained but claret-colored blots, a powerful odor like the smell of boiling mutton, and lower jaws spiked with teeth the size of my hand.

"We use the teeth, too," Mr. Murray told me when I found him at his home just down the road. "We send them to the Fiji Islands, where people consider them somewhat sacred, and a lot go to an American chap who does scrimshaw work. The carcass becomes high-protein animal food and fertilizer. The oil—about seven tons of it in a 42-foot whale—has any number of uses: in rust-proofing compounds, as a lubricant in watches and high-speed automotive transmissions, for softening leathers, and all through the chemical industry. The spermaceti and the wax go to the pharmaceutical industries. A lot of cosmetics contain ingredients that come from whales."

A CENTURY AND MORE AGO, whale hunters grossed grand fortunes on the seas around Australia. They came in blunt-nosed, square-sterned ships, some from Britain, many more from New England, and made a haven of the continent's southern end. Crewmen brawled and frolicked by the thousand through the eastern ports. When Australian pioneers of the 1840's ventured west to start a settlement on wild coastland not far from Albany, they found 23 Yankee whaling vessels riding at anchor off their intended campsite.

The industry began a slow decline in 1859 with the discovery of kerosene and a waning whale population. It continues today only under international restrictions made to save the great sea animals from extinction. Bad hunting closed down three shore stations in the early 1960's. That left Albany the last Australian port still in the business.

Extinction had already claimed a tiny land animal called the freckled marsupial mouse, naturalists believed, until wildlife photographer M. K. Morecombe found one early in 1967 some 30 miles east of Albany. Sometimes known by the Aboriginal name, dibbler—or in Latin, *Antechinus apicalis*—the insectivore had vanished from notice for 83 years. Only its nocturnal habits had kept it concealed, though. After the first sighting, people found more of the little creatures living in the area, going about their business of hunting for insects around the cylindrical flowers of small banksia plants.

ALBANY PILOT JOHN BELL took a break from his usual job of spotting whales for chaser ships and flew me east along a roadless coast. Skimming over farms and scrubland, writhing rivers, and rocky hunch-backed hills, we landed at Esperance, a quiet seaside community of 5,000 citizens that recently became something of a boomtown.

The town itself shows few signs of an economic surge. It looks, instead, like a restful ocean resort, which indeed it is. Homes and hostels built of brick, fiberboard, and corrugated metal stand along a beachside street, with windows watching waves frisk over an island-studded bay. But green-hulled grain ships tied up to a wharf hint of more importance to visitors who don't know that Esperance is the center of one of the biggest farm development projects in the world.

It began with scientific research. Less than two decades ago, the flat, sandy plains around the town supported sheep—one to every couple of acres—and very little else of use to man. But banksia thrived there, gnarled branches holding up drab red, pink, and yellow flowers. So did other vegetation strange to foreign eyes and ears: mallee scrub, munji and chittick plants, blackboy trees with tousled heads of leaves that look like wild grass.

Why did the land resist useful crops, agronomists wondered. The answer, applying to much Australian wasteland, lay in mineral deficiencies. But not great deficiencies; just a trace of a chemical element or two added to superphosphate fertilizer would make the soil bloom. Developers cleared the land of scrub, dragging railway tracks or chains behind their tractors. They spread five or ten pounds of zinc and copper per acre. Where the land needed molybdenum, two ounces could enrich that much land for ten years.

Sheep capacity leaped tenfold. Grain farmers reaped 15 bushels from each acre in the first planting. Today more than a million rich acres of farm- and sheepland reach away from Esperance. Investors—among them television personality Art Linkletter and financier David Rockefeller—add another 100,000 acres every year.

"One-fifth of Australia has a very high potential for development," agronomy professor Frank C. Crofts told me later at the University of Sydney. "Right now the country is bringing into production one to two million acres of land every year. Because of a national shortage of agricultural labor, we're developing land that Californians wouldn't bother with —low-fertility, low-rainfall areas. With good land, you've got to develop intensively to make it pay. But where the country's not so good, all you have to do is clear a little bit of natural vegetation, apply fertilizer, and put either wheat or stock on it. Generally speaking, for a new country our resources aren't easily won. But they're tremendous in size."

On a Sunday morning bus I sped 226 miles north, to the resources that brought Western Australia its first burst of prosperity. In semidesert country some 360 miles east of Perth, two prospectors hit a vein of gold in 1892. The strike was big. So were others that built a cluster of towns for many miles around.

I found Coolgardie, the first of the boomtowns, still alive but waning. Scrub covered the old football ground. Vacant lots yawned wide between scattered homes of fiberboard and metal. "There wouldn't be one-tenth of the crowd now that was in town when I was a lad," said taxi driver Tommy Langdon, who drove a sulky to school here in the 1920's. Today only grand orange limestone buildings on a wide and muddy main street hint of historic crowds and fortunes gained and spent.

But Australia still ranks fifth among the world's gold-producing countries. And most of the glittering wealth comes up from a honeycomb of

In quest of gold, miners of the 1850's hoist buckets of earth from diggings in Western Australia and empty them into a jiggling sluice box. Slots at the bottom trap the heavy metal, and water from the pump carries away the lighter tailings. In large part, Australia owes its existence as a nation to the waves of gold seekers who opened up the interior.

PHOTO RADIO TIMES HULTON PICTURE LIBRARY

mines some 23 miles northeast, around the city of Kalgoorlie. Tommy drove me there, through scrubland full of shanties, tents, and shafts of present-day prospectors. A mine official gave me overalls, steel-toed boots, and a helmet with a light. A double-deck cage elevator dropped us 1,853 feet underground.

It smelled like a damp basement—a dark tunnel in gray rock where the lamps on our heads waved lances of light through pale mist. Water dribbled from chinks overhead, glistening on the walls, leaving muddy pools

173

between steel rails on a floor of rock chips. We ducked to dodge log supports shoring up the ceiling. Where our tunnel met another, we hunched against a wall as lights like insect eyes came near and a battery-powered ore train rumbled past, the driver singing "I love coffee, I love tea..."

A transparent plastic tube wired to the ceiling led us toward a dragon's roar. Where the plump conduit emptied out its fresh air, a miner shut off his rock drill to show us gold.

"You see those little golden flecks?" he pointed. "That's not gold. It's pyrite. The color's a little different. And gold goes on sparkling when you turn your light to one side. Like this over here," he said, moving a few steps to the other wall of the tunnel. Free-gold specks the size of pinheads glittered in the rock like gems. "You can't see it always. A lot of the gold we haul out of here is too fine to be visible."

And almost too fine to be worked, Assistant Underground Manager Frank Lubbock indicated when I came up to daylight and cool May air. We strolled along the city's mile of mines, among steel-girder elevator towers, black smokestacks, and enormous corrugated metal buildings where caldrons spilled out molten gold syrup to be cast as ingots.

In Western Australia, Frank explained, surface workings often give the richest yields. Dryness is responsible for that. Much of the water in the earth seeps upward, bringing the precious metal with it. The higher levels of Kalgoorlie mines held the purest natural gold the world has ever seen.

"Now we're operating down to 4,000 feet," he said. "The mines stay open on government subsidy. What we'd like is a rise in the price of gold. That's no simple matter, of course. With gold used to back paper currencies and pay international debts, changes in its value affect world economics. But the official price has remained fixed at 35 American dollars per troy ounce since 1934, and the cost of mining it has been rising all the time. We gold miners are poor folk these days," he smiled. "Why, we've got miles of just-below-grade stuff we can't afford to touch."

A TREMENDOUS EXPANSE of land untouched — much of it virtually untouchable — sprawled ahead of a train I boarded at Kalgoorlie. Until 1917, when the Trans-Australian Railway huffed across the bottom of the continent for the first time, the country was impassable as well. Travelers heading east caught ships in Fremantle, rolling across the arc of heaving ocean called the Great Australian Bight to the port of Adelaide.

The rail journey, too, seemed strangely like a voyage at sea. Twin diesel engines ticking at the head of 14 cars roared to life. Steel wheels clunked over chinks in the track and then began a quick metallic gallop. From then on the train meant life itself for everyone on board. In the luxury of wood-paneled walls and floral carpets, piped music and conditioned air, the little colony of some 150 passengers and 33 crewmembers pounded into a thousand-mile ocean of empty country.

From an observation lounge in the last car, I watched a landscape of trees and shrubs recede behind us. Soil under the single set of tracks changed from tan to orange and then maroon and back again every dozen miles. Each color held pools and streaks of water. "The country's certainly

Freckled marsupial mouse, or dibbler, known only in Australia, stalks a grasshopper perched atop a flowering banksia. Once believed extinct, the nocturnal Antechinus apicalis *reappeared in Western Australia in 1967. Banksias perpetuate the name of Joseph Banks, botanist aboard Captain Cook's* Endeavour *in the 1770's. Later he wrote of "the fertility and salubrity of the climate," and recommended settlement of Australia.*

JAY H. MATTERNES

had its face washed," said a woman next to me. A phenomenal amount of rain had fallen in the past month or so. Kalgoorlie had almost an inch in a day. The Gibson Desert far to the north was blotched with shallow lakes.

I watched more rain come. Cumulonimbus clouds piled up like mounds of whipped cream. A bush of lightning burst ahead and shivered between earth and sky. Thunder rumbled like cannonballs on a stone staircase. Then the rain rushed down, a hail of silver arrows poking little craters into earth as sticky as glue.

"I've never seen the country look so good in my time," an elderly train steward remarked after the storm passed. It looked lush: grass and salt-bush pale green and a foot tall, healthy bluebush spraying up frosted leaves, big orange-trunked salmon gum trees waving little green tufts from the tips of upturned branches.

But it didn't last. Late that afternoon we hit the world's longest straight stretch of railway track — 297 miles long, to be exact. By that time we were charging over the Nullarbor Plain. "Nullarbor" — from Latin words meaning "no tree" — accurately describes the pan-flat limestone plateau that lacks enough topsoil to hold anything but shrubs. It won't hold rain either. The water drains through porous rock to underground lakes and rivers, some in huge caves still waiting for explorers. If you wandered 200 miles from west to east or 150 inland from the southern coastal cliffs, you'd find only haunting loneliness: a dead-flat vacant horizon, holes to the caverns blowing and sucking with every pressure change, and not a single plant rising above your knees.

The dingo fence rises taller, six feet, as a rule. In length, this wire-mesh barrier against the sheep-marauding wild dogs surely sets a world's record. It begins at the sea, where Western Australia touches the State of South

Australia. It met our railway line, followed it for awhile, then headed northeastward. On it goes, through dusty plains and harsh rock hills, over riverbeds and sand dunes. Turning onto scrubland, it ends in rich green hills of Queensland, some 150 miles from the east coast—almost 6,000 miles from where it began.

Maintenance workers live along the fence. They repair it when kangaroos or wild camels kick it down and dingoes bite holes in the wire. They rebuild it altogether when floods or shifting sands bury the mesh or leave it hanging like a volleyball net. Most of them have families in their isolated homesteads.

Maintenance crews live along the train line too. About nine o'clock at night, while passengers in the lounge car sang around a spinet piano, we stopped for some time at one of their villages, a place called Cook. On a single trackside street lighted by fluorescent bars, a couple of dozen clapboard homes stood in a rank, as identical as soldiers, each one story tall, each with a veranda.

Most of the villagers—railway workers, a teacher, a postal clerk, the keeper of the general store—slept behind dark windows. A few citizens had stayed up to give us water and fuel, and one, a little girl, ran from a house, carrying a big orange pneumatic rabbit to wave goodbye as the beat of the diesels began again.

Around 7 a.m. the sun burned up from the smooth, flat-topped Flinders Ranges, South Australia's most extensive chain of mountains. They begin at Port Pirie, an industrial city 136 miles north of Adelaide that treats the ore from Broken Hill in the world's largest lead-refining plant. They roll on past Port Augusta, 55 miles farther north, where I left the train after almost 28 hours aboard. Then, with mines and wheat and sheep around their slopes, the mountains heave 215 miles toward the dry and desolate heartland of Australia.

"**H**OLIDAY where the first human footprint could be yours!" a charter airplane firm in Port Augusta offers in its ads. Ever since imported camel drivers—usually from what is now Pakistan but always here called "Afghans"—moved northward with their caravans, transport to the continental center has jumped off from this town.

You can take a train, the Ghan—short for Afghan Express. Its 753-mile journey to the town of Alice Springs goes on for 30 hours. A tourist bus from Adelaide will bring you to the isolated mid-Australia settlement after a week of daylight jouncing on a dusty road where a two-way emergency radio aboard seems not the least superfluous. Or you can fill an automobile with water, spare parts, and nonperishable foods and drive the route yourself.

Driving, people told me, holds a minimum of dangers nowadays, if the driver stocks his mind with common-sense precautions. So what better way to go exploring where the first human footprint could be mine?

Towering karri tree, found only in southwest Australia, rivals redwoods in size and value, and yields durable timber ideal for wharves, bridges, and houses.

Faces of Perth: The town that switches on its lights for orbiting astronauts serves as capital of Western Australia and holds more than half the state's 893,000 people. Downtown, a newsboy (1) hawks the Saturday paper, a pensive lad (2) pauses on a street corner, and a young shopper (3) waits for a traffic signal. A spectator (4) at the Ascot Christmas Meet watches the posting of race results. Teen-agers on Cottesloe Beach (5) relax in the sun. Horse-racing fans (6) watch their favorites. A barefoot cricketer (7) swings mightily, and a fielder (8) waits for a hit. A matron (9) reflects quietly, and hippie motorcyclists (10) draw amused glances. A young racing enthusiast (11) looks over her shoulder at the crowd. Two chums (12) talk things over, and a sunbather (13) showers away sand. A ruddy-faced businessman (14) and a young swimmer (15) epitomize Australia's vigor. Fashions at the track: simple black and traditional tweed (16), and frilly headwear (17). Suzie Moncrieff, 1967's Miss Sunshine of Western Australia (18), deepens her tan. Perth, founded in 1829, grew slowly until the turn of the century, when gold discoveries in the interior attracted thousands of settlers to the town. Today their descendants enjoy the amenities of an industrialized society.

TOR EIGELAND, BLACK STAR

Feet braced on a listing deck, a crewman of the Messina *(opposite) hauls in a line attached to one of the vessel's crayfish pots, north of Perth. After wrestling the cane baskets aboard, the men pluck the crustaceans out, throwing back those not satisfying strict size requirements. The fishermen, predominantly immigrants from Yugoslavia and Italy, call the creatures crayfish, as do many other Australians; importers in the U.S.—where nearly all the catch reaches market—call them lobsters.*

181

Pounding through heavy seas, Cheynes III *pursues a sperm whale surfacing off Albany. Capt. Cheslyn Stubbs (above) stands ready at the harpoon gun, his eyes on the blowing whale's plume of spray. Sleek leviathans winched onto a slip (below) yield oil for lubricants and scores of other products, as well as waxes for cosmetics and candles.*

Bottlebrush, one of some 6,000 species of wild flowers in Western Australia, grows in needlelike clusters, flourishing along watercourses and in clay depressions on the south and east coasts. Aborigines soak the nectar-rich Callistemon *in water for a sugary drink.*

Kangaroo paws, shaped like the feet of their namesakes, thrive in low, wet spots in the state's southwest corner. In spring, regiments of the Anigozanthos—*a relative of the Easter lily—burst forth in greens, reds, browns, yellows, and even black.*

184

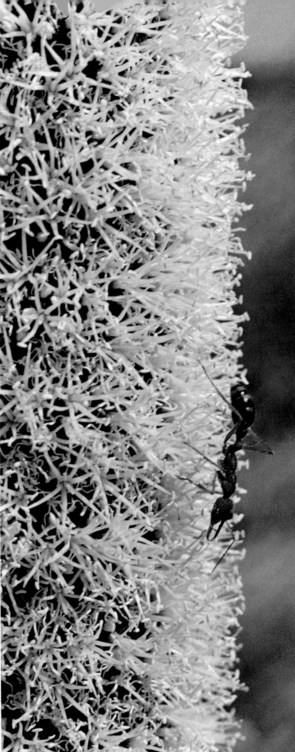

Dainty white petals of the Agonis
(upper) speckle large areas of Western
Australia, where 11 species of the showy
shrub bloom. The fringed lily (Thysanotus),
found in woodland areas during the
spring months between September and
December, wears fragile lavender lace.

Bulldog ant gathers nectar along the
flower spike of a blackboy. Thick trunk
and broomstick spike rise as high as
18 feet, looking in the distance somewhat
like a man with a spear. Xanthorrhoea,
averaging an inch of growth a year,
flowers infrequently, usually after a bushfire.

185

*Christmas tree, decorated with cadmium
orange flowers, heralds December. A
member of the parasitic mistletoe family,
Nuytsia feeds on the roots of other
plants, reaching a height of 35 feet. Some
call it the "doctor's friend" because
the brittle branches break easily under
the weight of climbing children.*

RON YOUNGER (LOWER RIGHT) AND RICHARD WOLDENDORP

Prickly Dryandra *(upper)
flourishes on gravelly hillsides near
Albany and in the Stirling Range.
The shrub's 50 species grow only in
Western Australia. Sturt's desert pea
(Clianthus), named for explorer
Charles Sturt, sprouts only in
the continent's arid regions.*

Australia's national emblem, the wattle (Acacia), *appears in all the states and on the coat of arms. Its 600 species range from small shrubs to large trees, some so rich in flowers that Australians call them "golden rain." Settlers named the trees after seeing Aborigines interweave—or wattle—the branches into crude shelters.*

Red flowering gum, *one of several hundred species of* Eucalyptus *that range from the parched center to the sandy coast, thrives in the southwest corner of Western Australia. Commonly called gum trees, Australia's widely transplanted native eucalypts now grow in more than 70 countries, providing valuable hardwood timber.*

Late afternoon sun gilds Kalgoorlie with the color of the gold that lies beneath the city. In 1893 Irish prospector Paddy Hannan stumbled upon the lode here; miners from all over the world soon followed. The area has since yielded ore worth nearly $1,173,000,000, and now accounts for 65 percent of Australia's annual production of $25,000,000. In the vaults of the Australian and New Zealand Bank, manager Sam Willis wheels two weeks' output—bars valued at $400,000. On Hannan Street, named for Paddy, a car heeds an explicit traffic direction. Businessmen pause before a sign offering relief from the heat. Situated in near-desert, the town must pipe its water 350 miles from the Mundaring reservoir near Perth.

More precious than gold, Western Australia's farms and stock stations surpass all its mines in the production of wealth, sending food to markets around the world. In the southwest part of the state, cattle graze and hayers load bales of feed. A truck (left) bears drums of liquid fertilizer. The state strives to open up a million acres of new land a year by adding nutrients to the mineral-deficient soil.

The Center: Journey
Into Alice's Wonderland

BRUCE BRANDER

ROCKETS ROAR on Australia's wild frontier. Wild indeed the land remains, hardly touched by the hand of man. For most of a day I drove north from Port Augusta to reach the missile-launching base of Woomera. Beyond a few railroad towns, I saw no life but desiccated scrub and bouncing kangaroos. Anywhere along the way on a very hot day a man could die of thirst within nine hours.

Then, near the spot where Gulliver discovered the Kingdom of Lilliput, "... North-west of *Van Diemen's* Land ... in the Latitude of 30 Degrees 2 Minutes South," I entered the region where experimental rockets begin their fiery journey farther northwest across the continent.

A tall wire fence guards the town of Woomera from marsupials and unofficial observers. But a pass allows a visitor to step off the desert into an oasis of comfortable living. The scientific settlement of 5,000 people took its name from the long stick called a woomera that helps the Aboriginal hunter hurl his spears with greater speed and power. But it takes its notion of how men should live from faraway sophisticated cities.

Water from the distant Murray River arrives through a pipe in plentiful supply, doing away with the need for salty local bore-water. All supplies, from furniture to ice cream — some 350 tons a week — come by air, road, and train from Adelaide, 300 miles south.

For several hours I used my limited government permit to tour neat

Red kangaroo on the central desert pauses in the shadow of a pole supporting telegraph and telephone wires that span the continent between Adelaide and Darwin. First strung in the 1870's, the 1,973-mile line linked Australia with an undersea cable to provide rapid communication with other areas of the world.

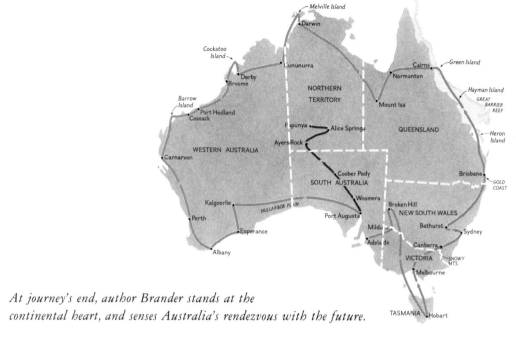

Melville Island
Darwin
Cockatoo Island
Kununurra
Cairns — Green Island
Normanton
Derby
Broome
NORTHERN
TERRITORY
Hayman Island
GREAT BARRIER REEF
Barrow Island
Port Hedland
Cossack
Mount Isa
Papunya
Alice Springs
QUEENSLAND
Heron Island
Ayers Rock
WESTERN AUSTRALIA
Carnarvon
Coober Pedy
SOUTH AUSTRALIA
Brisbane
GOLD COAST
Kalgoorlie
NULLARBOR PLAIN
Woomera
Broken Hill
NEW SOUTH WALES
Perth
Port Augusta
Mildura
Bathurst
Sydney
Esperance
Adelaide
Canberra
Albany
VICTORIA
SNOWY MTS.
Melbourne
TASMANIA
Hobart

At journey's end, author Brander stands at the continental heart, and senses Australia's rendezvous with the future.

green streets with quiet bungalows and brick apartment blocks, to lunch at the shopping center and cool off at an olympic-size swimming pool. But long before dark, I plunged into the open wilderness again.

"Leave your women behind when you come to Coober Pedy," I've often heard seasoned outback travelers warn. After a 15-hour drive to the rustic town, I understood what they meant. Men, and only men, scuffed along a dusty, stony street, fetching bread from a bakery, buying bananas, shovels, and explosives at the Miners Store Ltd.

The name of the place, in the language of a local tribe, means "white-fella's burrow." White- or dark-skinned, any fellow can stake a claim for 50 cents and burrow a hole in red, pink, and mustard-hued soil. If he's intensely lucky, he'll find a streak or fat pocket of dazzling, multicolored opal. More than a hundred free-lance miners fossick for the gemstone through the blazing summers. In the cool of winter, a thousand and more try their luck among the largest opal fields in the world.

With no baths allowed for lack of water, I stayed in one of the two motels that rose in recent years near a drive-in theater and a beer hall. Citizens spent the night underground, where most of the town hides, in cosy hand-hewn homes in the hillsides that keep the scorching sun at bay and save the cost of truck-delivered building materials.

Explorers cursed the gibber plains. I understood why as I jounced north at 30 miles an hour. With sun smashing down and the breeze blasting by at 120° F. or more, they walked for days over gibber stones, sometimes small but here the size of fists. Flat, the land lies, dull orange from end to end with not a tree in sight — an ankle-twisting anguish of monotony.

The first explorers, seeking the vast inland sea their flights of logic had devised, found nothing more than infinite illusory mirages. Yet maps of this country still make big blue claims for water. Lake Eyre, for example, 130 miles east of the road, blotches some 3,000 square miles of space. In 1950 unusual rains filled the basin for the first time in living memory. Go there now and you'll probably find a crust of pink-white salt thick enough to support a locomotive.

Sometimes for lunch and usually to sleep, I stopped at cattle stations. Welbourn Hill maintained a small restaurant for travelers passing through. Victory Downs offered immaculate motel rooms, a general store, a dining hall, and a prefabricated bar next to the homestead. All the way to Alice Springs, a traveler finds a comfortable place to stay at least every dozen hours.

But what do you do if your car breaks down? Stay with it, local people warn. Walking in this land of wide horizons without a nearby goal brings quick exhaustion, sometimes death. But on the road, help may come. One day I counted a dozen cars and trucks moving on the road. Now and then station hands roar by on lightweight motorcycles, heading out to round up cattle, or to shoot a herd of brumbies—wild horses—that devour precious pasturage. Several times I met Aboriginal stockmen loping along the road on horseback in bright shirts and headbands like those once worn by Plains Indians. If no one happens by and drinkable provisions trickle down to nothing, drain the water from the radiator.

THE LAND itself hides sly supplies of moisture. A line of trees tells of a riverbed. It may look dry as a bacon rind. But find a bend and dig. If a bar of rock caused the turn, water will fill the hole months after a rain. Wide-spreading coolabah trees growing 80 feet tall usually cling to such river courses; if you see one elsewhere, water lies not far beneath.

Somewhere along the way, you should stop your car, get out, and turn your back on the road—just walk a short distance away. Scuffing between wild flowers and thorny shrubs, you sense hours of engine whine and metallic clatter fading from the ears of memory. Hearing grows acute. You listen, with effort, to utter silence.

A breeze whispers. Dry scrapes come from the shivering tips of low acacia trees. Fish-shaped eucalyptus leaves rub together overhead, and it seems the air is telling secrets.

A mile from the road you quite possibly plant a first human footprint on dusty ground. A pair of kangaroos soaking up the gray shade of a desert oak tree not far away find this genuinely remarkable. They throw their weight back on heavy tails and strain their necks to see, little forepaws touching like hands offering a prayer. Stand still as a stone and they might swivel forward to munch at a tussock, or flop down on their sides in a luxury of relaxation. A quick step sends them bounding off, but only to a safer vantage point.

What an extraordinary feeling to stand alone out here! As far as the horizon and farther beyond that the world lies flat, except, perhaps, for a clump of hills crouched at the edge of sky like worn stone lions in an ancient park. When the breeze dies, quiet turns absolute. The sun flares, baking earth and plants. Nothing moves. And so the day slips on like any other in the past million years.

In the harsh and untamed center of Australia, Alice Springs thrives with the sort of cheery optimism that promises to make a town a city.

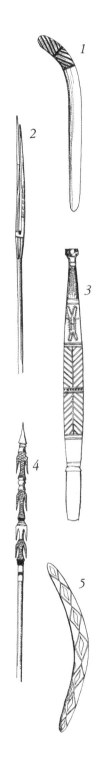

The settlement began modestly. In the 1870's, the transcontinental telegraph wire touched here from Adelaide, 981 miles south, and zipped on to Darwin, 954 miles north. Near a broad freshwater spring named Alice for the wife of superintendent of telegraphs Charles Todd, workers set up a rustic relay station.

The Alice, or simply Alice, as Australians know the town, enlarged with equal modesty. Cattlemen willing to endure five dry years for every verdant season—though sometimes things got worse—stocked stations that eventually spread for 200 miles and more around. Yet hardly half a hundred people lived in the settlement when the Central Australian Railway pushed up this far in 1929.

The town boomed only during recent decades, its population leaping from 1,000 in the late 1930's to the present 8,000. Why? Well, for one thing, the cattle trade has grown. In a good year, 40,000 head bellow onto rail wagons for the journey south. That explains the banks and saddle shops on Todd Street, and fluorescent-lighted pubs where stockmen in muddy cowboy boots stomp out inventive steps to pop music on weekend nights.

But, strolling along the shady length of Todd Street, one begins to wonder what accounts for the stores with city fashions, fresh vegetables and milk, new magazines, cookies from Vienna, Danish caviar, and a great deal more the outback isn't used to. And what spurred the growth for block after block of comfortable new bungalows tucked neatly within green lawns and beds of English flowers? Along with oil explorations and the settlement's job of transport and supply, tourism has turned the Alice from a cowtown to a place of prosperity and polish. Metropolitan Australians always liked their outback land. But for generations city-bred citizens rarely ventured very far or very often into the wilds "back o' beyond." Now vacationists strike inland by the thousand. Many of these thousands, joined by foreign visitors, come to Alice, an unusually pleasant outback spot accessible by road, train, and jet.

They soak up the restorative peace of semidesert solitude. They bask away the months of winter in a climate that offers all the comforts of the season in Arizona or Morocco—nippy sleeping weather at night and bright, warm afternoons. And they venture out from new hotels with swimming pools for jaunts into the wonderland of wilderness where Alice lives.

The reddish-orange sandstone Macdonnell Ranges ripple past the town on a 250-mile course across the Northern Territory. Scoured by the gritty winds of eons, the pleated ridge lumps along like the backbone of some enormous prehistoric monster, hiding yawning gaps, a valley full of

Intricate patterns embellish the weapons of Aborigines. The fluted boomerang (1), once used in intertribal fighting, can cut open a man's stomach; two such throwing sticks become musical instruments when clapped together. Arnhem Land fishermen carry pronged spears (2). The woomera (3), used to cradle a spear for throwing, provides added leverage. Eight barbs project from a eucalyptus wood spear (4). A diamond motif decorates a boomerang (5) from northern New South Wales.

Eyes on his quarry, a hunter tenses to hurl a nonreturning boomerang. The throwing stick can kill or disable a kangaroo 200 feet away. Many Aborigines still go on hunts, but firearms increasingly replace traditional weapons. The dingo, Australia's wild dog, sometimes helps when domesticated by chasing game to exhaustion.

DRAWINGS BY RICHARD SCHLECHT

rare *Livistona mariae* palms, and gorges where sunlight seldom reaches strollers at the bottom.

A nearby ghost town called Arltunga, a dude ranch Australian style, and Aboriginal settlements—all within a day's drive—offer city-bred visitors handy glimpses of life in the wilds. And some 10,000 travelers a year from all over the world take the jaunt by air or road to Ayers Rock, a feldspar-rich sandstone outcrop, 1,143 feet high, sprawling on an eerie, vacant plain like a monstrous beached whale.

Four hundred miles by air passes for a casual sightseeing trip out here. For the Royal Flying Doctor Service based at Alice Springs, distances like that are all in a day's work.

A missionary named John Flynn pioneered Australia's outback medical clinic in the 1920's. Today his nonprofit lifesaving network maintains radio stations and air service throughout sparsely settled areas.

"The Alice is one of 13 control stations," Base Director George Brown told me in a radio building not far from Todd Street. "Our territory? Oh, it covers about 440,000 square miles. We call into 82 ports. The farthest one is Balbirini cattle station 530 miles north-northeast.

"A great part of our work is emergency evacuation," said Brown, a Scotsman and former British Merchant Navy radio officer. "This month has been busy—nearly one evacuation every day. In a year, we can count on 100,000 miles of emergency flying. Not all of our work is emergency, though. We make routine clinical flights—about 80,000 miles a year. And for cases not severe enough to require evacuation, we diagnose the trouble and prescribe home treatment during radio clinics held every day."

All through the outback, I had seen home treatment kits—bush pharmacies holding sedatives and antibiotics, scalpels, forceps, and tourniquets, more than 80 items identified by number and name.

"Between clinics," Brown added, "we read telegrams too. For many of these people, we are virtually the only link with the outside world."

But not all station-dwellers live in constant solitude. Private planes and four-wheel-drive vehicles put many of them within shopping range of a sizable community. In a small truck, a stock agent named Ian Millard drove me westward to the 1,450-square-mile Hamilton Downs station, holding the speedometer at 60 miles an hour all the way.

Bill Prior and his wife Dawn, who have managed the property since 1957, met us at the homestead. They led us past a mechanic's shed into a fenced square where quonset-style stockmen's quarters huddled among shade trees near their white sheet-metal home.

"We drive into town once a week," Bill said over a lunch of beef and potatoes in a kitchen as large as most modern living rooms. "But between trips I reckon you could say we live like other station folk. We have an emergency airstrip and an R.F.D.S. radio. Our boys go to boarding school. And our daughter Wendy gets her lessons by correspondence and the School of the Air."

Bill drove me over part of the property's 60-mile length. "We normally run 7,500 head," he said as our white utility truck dodged mulga and iron-wood trees, low acacias and termite mounds. "The land is rated at five beasts to the square mile. In a good year we'd turn off 2,000 cattle." We jounced over gnarled fallen logs and ruts. Wiry scrub screeched against steel sides. "The property might gross $150,000 in a good year, half that in mediocre times, with expenses running around $50,000. You can make big profit in this country. But you can cop a big loss too."

In a nine-year drought that began in 1957, stations in the district lost so heavily that some owners put their land up for sale. Agronomists began to recommend abandonment for ten good years to let the earth recover. But rains of 1966 found seeds under the soil far hardier than even experts had expected. Within 15 months, the land turned greener than most people could remember.

Even in verdant years the dangers of a semidesert hold deadly threats for travelers. "It's serious business when people get lost out there," Constable Anthony Stenhouse told me at the one-story Northern Territory Police station in town. The young lawman added a slouch hat to his neat brown wool uniform and showed me outside to meet one of the men who finds them.

Bill Edaminja, an Aboriginal tracker, can read in the vaguest trail of a car, an emu, or a man the details that printing in a book might hold. "A track—it tell a story," he explained. "You see a fella's face, you know that fella; his track, you know more."

"It's really amazing how they do it," Constable Stenhouse added. "They can tell how old a track is. They can tell the difference between a white man, a half-caste, and a full-Aborigine by the way he walks. Very often they know what tribe a person belongs to, the age, the sex, the state of health, and sometimes who the person is before we find him."

Not long ago—just a few years in some cases—their lives depended on such skills. As adapted to the land as the eucalypt, Aborigines could find sustenance almost anywhere in the continent's doubting heart. Even today, you can watch them conjure food from bleak, ferocious country.

Witchetty grubs: Women with long pointed digging sticks scrape away soil from the foot of an acacia bush; they crack open roots; from some they pull the squirming white larvae of wood-boring beetles, the larger ones about as long and as thick as a man's forefinger; they eat them alive, tasting a delicate flavor sometimes compared to whipped cream.

Honey: Women walk and examine the ground, slackening pace when they sight a file of yellow-spotted ants; they follow the chain to a tiny hole and dig; some three feet down, galleries of an insect city yield heaping handfuls of translucent amber storage ants the size and shape of small marbles, each fat with sweet, warm honey held in the abdomen for the colony's later use.

Kangaroo, emu: Men with boomerangs, notched spears, and woomeras track several hundred yards apart; with the silence of the hunter, they converse in an eloquent language of hand signs; an animal in sight, they freeze, stand motionless until it looks away; a boomerang swishes, the creature looks up; spearmen spring forward and hurl for the kill.

DURING THE RECENT DROUGHT, the last known groups of nomads trickled in to church missions and government settlements to accept the more assured livelihood the white man offers. Some wandered in by themselves. Motorized patrols found others, sighting "smokes" and rumbling through trackless wilderness to reach campfires before the people who built them moved on.

With Alan Jackson, owner of Drive Yourself Landrovers Pty. Ltd., I traveled westward from Alice Springs to see the dark-skinned desertmen adapting to the frontier that came out to meet them.

Raw rock ridges roasted in the sun to either side as we rolled down a bitumen highway not quite wide enough for two cars. Crowds of pink-and-gray galahs fluttered across the road, some nearly hitting the windshield. High above, flocks of green budgerigars soared against hard blue sky in formations as trim as a kite.

Pavement ended and the Land-Rover whined at 50 miles an hour over dusty bulldozed earth. Five extra leaves that Alan had added to the standard nine-leaf front springs braced the wheels for washouts—trenches carved from watercourses hours after a rain begins. One I saw later dropped down eight feet. Also in precaution, the vehicle carried a ten-gallon water tank and "kangaroo bars," stout steel pipes that most out-back-dwellers weld in front of the radiator to guard against the consequences of collision with animals.

All day we drove, then long after dark. In the broom of light that swept the road ahead, we watched the busy nightlife of the outback—hopping mice, a rock python, lizards, orange-reflecting eyes of cattle. With a mild wind, beige balls of tumbleweed—called roly-poly here—bounced by. A calm brought a light flurry of white moths. Passing through cattle gates, we stopped to camp well within Papunya Aboriginal Reserve.

"A six-dog night," people here would call the frosty darkness of this season, when Aborigines gather domesticated dingoes around them for warmth. Under three blankets and a sheet of canvas, I felt too cold to sleep. Grass whispered. Distant insects sounded like the creaking of great trees. I roused Alan when two wild horses galloped by, coats gleaming in the light of a half-moon. An owl flapped low with a whistling sound to investigate our waning fire. I dozed and woke up shivering. A kangaroo exhaled a pant and thumped away into the night. Near dawn a dingo roused me with its scratching at the earth. It trotted on with the calm urgency of a shooting gallery figure, searching the dark with Oriental eyes.

Papunya, one of 14 Aboriginal Reserves in the Northern Territory, is part of a spread of tribal country that reaches over 44,800 square miles, mostly sandy land where eucalypts grow sparsely amid spinifex grass. Nearly 1,000 people live there: Walbiri, Pintubi, and Luritja tribesmen, Aranda, Pitjantjara, and Waramunga.

SUPERINTENDENT Russell E. Nicholas met us at the small government settlement, a village of large silvery corrugated metal huts and clapboard buildings rising high on stilts. He took me first to the western outskirts of the village where Pintubi tribesmen, some only 18 months off the desert, lived in leafy windbreaks the size and shape of pup tents.

"We believe these are the last of the fully independent nomads," Nicholas said, "though there may be a few more out there," he added with a nod toward the wilderness. "We still send out patrols from time to time." New arrivals first receive clothing, he explained. The local hospital staff trains mothers to feed their children regularly. Youngsters attend school. Teen-agers learn handicrafts. And men go to work at regular jobs: kitchen tasks, road-making, fencing, and cattle-raising. "Everything that's done here amounts to a training program," Nicholas said as we drove back toward town.

We passed a lean, hard Pintubi who sat cross-legged in the road playing with a tiny girl. He looked at us with no expression, no apparent interest, but the child smiled. A file of barefoot girls in cotton frocks and woolen sweaters marched along the wide, dusty settlement street. Boys in gray school uniforms tussled on a patch of lawn while a few others sprawled out in warming sun to read. "Our final aim," Nicholas said, "is to train the people so they'll be able to live as part of the national community. Integration is the word for it."

Integration seemed the word for all the great endeavors my co-authors and I had witnessed in Australia. Just as well-planned efforts bring Aborigines and white Australians closer, so do mining booms, stupendous irrigation schemes, and agricultural research integrate sophisticated cities ever more closely with a vast and vacant frontier. A few prophetic scholars already envision the continent fully settled. The Australian nation, they proclaim, could grow 80,000,000 strong and spread rich productivity from coast to coast. But visionary hopes get only passing notice from Australians of today. They are too busy for dreaming, with the plans and the tasks that build grand dreams.

Drillers clear debris from a well casing ruptured by water pressure at Coward Springs, 400 miles north of Adelaide. Artesian flows keep stock ponds filled.

Suddenly rich, Greek-Australian opal miners rest in 110-degree heat in a metal hut at Coober Pedy as their smiling backer John Asikas dishes up dinner. Asikas drove 590 miles inland from Adelaide over desert roads to hear firsthand how members of the Stefanapoulos family discovered a vein of opal after six months of digging. At top right, Peter unwraps explosives, and brother George prepares wiring for a mine blast. Inside the shaft, cousin Nick watches as George works a nodule loose from sandstone. Until 1963, George made a meager living gathering resin for wine making in Nauplion, Greece; now he shares in gemstones like the one opposite—worth $40 to $50 per carat. Although prospectors have dug at Coober Pedy since 1915, valuable deposits still turn up occasionally. At left, Nick looks into the mirror at a lucky man.

Chattering galahs (opposite) settle on leafless branches as the sun drops low in a yellow-hot sky near Lake Eyre. Desert-conditioned birds of the "Red Centre" drink from water holes fed by salty artesian springs. The cold silver dawn awakens crested doves (above), and presses light into the breasts of gray teal drowsing in the shallows.

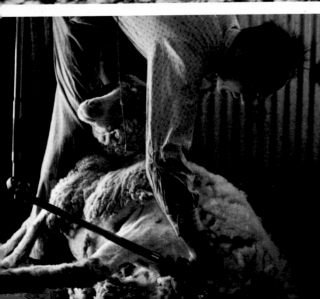

Home on the gibber plain: Half-finished after 13 lean years, the house of Hugh and Laurel Frahn dry-roasts near a tree-shaded creek-bed on Copper Hills sheep station. Going it alone, Frahn shears one of 1,200 Merinos that scour 216 square miles for grass. On the porch, their School of the Air classroom, the children nap and play in scant shade. A tank stores drinking water. Big pleasure for a young Aussie: nuzzling his 18-month-old pet joey.

Flying Doctor Michael Green talks by telephone at Port Augusta into a two-way radio network connecting him with 3,800 desert-dwellers. He prescribes pills from numbered bottles in home kits, and goes by plane on house calls as far away as 400 miles. During clinic hours at Port Augusta Hospital (opposite), he examines an Aborigine baby. Below, in a flying ambulance, a patient tells Dr. Green her symptoms.

Like a green arrow on the yellow desert, Alice Springs points south to Heavitree Gap, gateway through the 250-mile-long Macdonnell Ranges. Some 8,000 people live in "the Alice," at the center of the continent, drawing their water from underground basins that fill during flash-floodings of the normally dry Todd River (left). Twice a week, a train hauls cattle 981 miles from end-of-the-line Alice to Adelaide and returns with supplies. At the freight yard just north of Billy Goat Hill (top center) a crane (below) transfers cargo to truck trailers. Such "road trains" enter the Stuart Highway near the oval playing field (foreground) of Anzac Hill School, then swing north for stops along the route to Darwin, 954 miles away. Alice, no longer remote, attracts some 20,000 visitors a year; most arrive at the jet airport beyond the gap.

Residents of the Hermannsburg Aboriginal Mission sit on a veranda at the settlement, 84 miles west of Alice Springs; initials on a wide hatband identify a member of the village council. At right, a young cattle hand accompanies his son home on nearby Papunya, a government reserve. At a manual-arts center there, 13-year-old Victor Jungari learns to operate a sanding machine, an early step toward a job in the future.

A sphinx in the central desert, the red mass of Ayers Rock juts 1,143 feet out of a sandy plain about 200 air miles southwest of Alice Springs. The astonished discoverer, W. C. Gosse, sighted the 2¼-mile length of the feldspar-rich arkose outcrop in 1873, and named it for Sir Henry Ayers, then Premier of South Australia. Uptilted eons ago from an ancient seabed, the stratified rock resembles some mythical animal huddled in deep sleep, its smooth red skin scratched by clawings of rain and wind. Aborigines believed their first ancestors, semi-human heroes of the Dreamtime, or Creation, did in fact rest on the mound in the form of stones and boulders. For the desert nomads, every crevice, stain, rock stratum, and stone recorded an incident in the mighty deeds of the hare-wallaby men, poisonous-snake people, and other mythical beings who created landscape, laws, and tribal rituals. Until recent decades, the Pitjantjara tribe carried out manhood and fertility rites in sacred caves around the base of the monolith. Faded wall paintings illustrating Aboriginal myths now intrigue thousands of sightseers who fly or go overland to the Rock each year. The visiting ritual includes walking the seven-mile road around the mass, snapping pictures of the startling changes in its color at sunset—from fiery red to delicate mauve—and perhaps climbing to the top. From there, visitors look down on red dunes softened by a cover of spinifex, eucalypts, mulgas, and desert oaks. Beyond a waste of sand ridges they see the domes of Mount Olga, 20 miles distant, and gaze deep into the heart of wild, difficult, strangely beautiful Australia.

TED SPIEGEL, RAPHO GUILLUMETTE

Index

Illustrations references appear in *italics*.

Aborigines 12, 21, 126, 128, 146-147, 151, 159, 162, 187, 195, *208;* Art *142,* 147, 214; Beliefs and rituals 214; Corroboree 128, *141;* Education *142,* 147, 200, *212;* Fishermen *141;* Food 142, 147, 184, 198-199; Hunters 124, 147, 193, *197;* Origins 146; Population 142, 147; Reserves and settlements 141, *142,* 146-147, 197, 199, 200, *212;* Stockmen 99, *121,* 124, 131, *138;* Trackers 198; Tribes 146-147, 200; Wars 100, Weapons 193, *196, 197,* 199
Acacia 187
Adelaide, S.A. 21-24, *30-32,* 169, 174, 176, 193, 196, 200, 202, 211; Population 22
Afghan Express 176
Agonis 185
Agricultural research 50-51
Agriculture: Barossa Valley *21,* 24; Murray River Valley 25-26, *35,* 49; Queensland 99-100, 121, 123; Tasmania 27, *42;* Western Australia *18-19,* 145, 149, 150, *156-157,* 172; *see also* Cattle; Sheep; Sugar cane
Albany, W.A. 171, 172, 183, 186
Alice Springs, N.T. 128, 176, 195-196, 197, 199, *211,* 212, 214; History 196; Population 211
Amitermes meridionalis 137
Antechinus apicalis 172, *175*
Anzac 52, 145; Anzac Day 145-146
Anzac Parade, Canberra *63*
Arafura Sea 148
Archibald Memorial Fountain, Sydney *83*
Area of Australia 9, 10, 11
Arltunga, N.T. 197
Arnhem Land, N.T. 128, 196
Artesian basins 125, 128; Springs *204;* Well *200*
Asikas, John *202*
Askin, Robin William, Premier (New South Wales) 72
Astronomy 52
Atherton Tableland, Qld. 121
Australian and New Zealand Bank, Kalgoorlie: Vaults *188*
Australian Dried Fruits Association 25
Australian National University, 52
Australian War Memorial, Canberra, 52, *63*
Australian Wool Board 47
The Australian Ugliness (Boyd) 46
Ayers, Sir Henry 214
Ayers Rock, N.T. 197, *214*

Back Perisher Mountain, N.S.W. *66*
Balbirni, cattle station, N.T. 197
Ballarat, Vic. 46
Balmain, N.S.W. 70
Banks, Joseph *175*
Banksia 172, *175*
Barkly Highway, Qld.-N.T. 128
Barossa Valley, S.A.: Wine-

making *20,* 24
Barrier Industrial Council 26
Barrier Ranges, N.S.W. 26
Barrow Island, W.A. 152; Oil industry 152, *162*
Barwick, Sir Garfield 73
Bass Strait, Tas.-Vic. 28, 47
Bathurst, N.S.W. 75
Bathurst Island, N.T. 141
Bauxite 102
Belair National Park, S.A. 24
Bendigo, Vic. 45
Bennelong Point, Sydney 69, *78*
Billy Goat Hill, Alice Springs *211*
Birds 103, 148, 199;
    Crested doves *204;*
    Galahs *165, 199, 204;* Gray teal *204;*
    Lorikeets *108;* Magpie geese 148-149;
    Reef heron *116*
Blackboy trees 172, *185*
Blowering Dam, Tumut River *51, 64*
Blue Mountains, N.S.W. 75
Bondi Beach, Sydney *88*
Boomerangs 21, 142, *196, 197*
Botanic Gardens, Sydney 69, 71
Botany Bay, N.S.W. 10, 12, 146
Bottlebrush *184*
Bourke, Qld. 125
Bourke Street, Melbourne *45*
Boxing Day 70
Boyd, Robin 45
Boyd, Stan 104
Bradley Head, Sydney 12
Brisbane, Qld. 12, 21, 97-98, 100, 102, 104, *106;* Population 106
Brisbane River, Qld. *97, 106*
Broken Hill, N.S.W. 24, 26-27, *37-38* 123, 176
Broken Hill Proprietary Company Ltd. 47
Broome, W.A. 150-151, 159, 165; Population 159; School *159*
Brown, George 197
Buckley, Noel 47
Buffalo, water 128, *138*
Burley Griffin, Lake, Canberra 50, *63*
Burnet, Sir Macfarlane 56
Burnie, Tas. *42*

Cairns, Qld. 12, 103, 104, 121, 131
Callistemon 184
Camels *149,* 150, 176
Cameron, L.G. 25
Canberra, A.C.T. 49, 50, *51,* 51, 52, *63,* 64, 72
Canobie station, Qld. 127
Cape Leveque 151
Cape York Peninsula, Qld. 99, 104
Capitals: Federal *see* Canberra; Financial *see* Melbourne
Carnarvon, W.A.: Space tracking station 152, *166*
Carpentaria, Gulf of, Qld. 99, 102, 123, 132
Carpentaria Shire Council Chambers, Normanton *121, 132*
Casey, Lord (Richard Gardiner) *63,* 74
Cattle industry *95,* 97, 100, 104, 121, 123, 124, 126, 127-128, *131, 191,* 196, 198, 211; Buffalo 128, *138;* History 127
Central Australian Railway 196
Centre, the, region 12, *16*

195-200, 204
Chaffey, George 25
Chaffey, W.B. 25
Channel Country, Qld. 100
Cheynes Beach Whaling Company Proprietary Ltd. 171; Whaler *183*
Chinese 100, 148, 159
Clarence Strait, N.T. 147
Cleland National Park, S.A. 24
Christmas tree *186*
Clianthus 186
Climate 123, New South Wales 46; Northern Territory 145, 149, 196; Queensland 132, Brisbane 98; South Australia 194
Coal 102
Coat of arms *4*
Cockatoo Island, W.A.: Iron ore production 150, *152, 155*
Collins, Capt. W.E. 26
Colonial Sugar Refining Company building, Sydney 71
Commonwealth Scientific and Industrial Research Organisation (CSIRO) 51, 72, 74, 76
Coober Pedy, S.A. 194; Opal miners 194, *202*
Cook, Happy *142*
Cook, Capt. James 10, 11, 101, 103, 146; Ship *101,* 175
Cook, S.A. 176
Cook Highway, Qld. 104
Cooktown, Qld. 101, 104
Coolgardie, W.A. 173; Hotel *169*
Cooma, N.S.W. 49, *51*
Cooper 127, *135;* Smelter *135*
Copper Hills sheep station, S.A. *207*
Corroboree, Aboriginal celebration 128, *141*
Cossack, W.A. *165*
Costeo, Peter *156*
Cotton: Western Australia 150, *156-157*
Coulls, Allan 26
Coward Springs, S.A.: Water well *200*
Crayfishing *181*
Crocodiles 124, 132
Crofts, Frank C. 172
Cronulla, N.S.W. 51
Croydon, Qld. 123
Currumbin Bird Sanctuary, Gold Coast: Lorikeets *108*

Daintree River, Qld. 104
Dairying: Queensland 99
Dampier, W.A. 151; Ore-loading *155*
Dandenong Ranges, Vic. 47
Darling Downs, Qld. 99, 100
Darling Harbour, Sydney 70
Darling River, N.S.W. 24, 26, *38*
Darwin, N.T. 28, 127, 128, 137, 145-149, 150, 193, 196, 211
Denver City Hotel, Coolgardie *169*
Derby, W.A. 150
Derwent River, Tas. *40-41*
Deserts: Western Australia 150, 175
Dibbler 172, *175*
Dingo fence 175-176
Dingoes 124, 175-176, *197,* 199, 200
Domain, the, Sydney 74, *83*
Drought (1957-1966) 193
Dryandra 186

Eagle Farm Airport, Brisbane 97-98
Eggan, Dr. Olin 52
El Alamein Memorial Fountain, Sydney 71, 80
Elizabeth, S.A. 23, 24; Factory 32
Emu 4, 72
Endean, Dr. Robert 104
Endeavour, H.M. Bark 10, 101, 175
Engledow, L.W. 49
Esperance, W.A. 172
Eucalypts 18, 66, 108, 137, 171, 176, 187, 196
Eucumbene, Lake, N.S.W. 49, 51
Evans, Dr. Lloyd 51
Exmouth Gulf, W.A.: U. S. Navy communications base 152
Exports 47, 97, 106, 118, 159, 181, 191
Eyre, Edward John 23, 24
Eyre, Lake, S.A. 16, 194-195, 204

Farm Cove, Sydney 69, 74
Federal Council of Australasia 28
Festivals: Festival of Arts, Adelaide 22, 31; Surf carnival, Sydney 88; Waratah Festival, Sydney 84
Fishermen: Tiwi tribesmen 141
Fishing, commercial 181; see also Oyster farming; Whaling
Flemington Course, Melbourne 58-59
Flinders Ranges, S.A. 176
Flora 104, 122-123, 171, 172, 175, 184-187, 214; Banksia 171, 175; Eucalypts 18, 66, 108, 137, 171, 176, 187, 196; Palms 16, 171
Flynn, John 197
Frahn, Hugh and Laurel 207
Fremantle, W.A. 169, 170, 174
Frith, Dr. Harry 72

Galahs 74, 165, 199, 204
Gallipoli, Turkey 52, 74, 145
Geese, magpie 148-149
General Motors-Holden's Pty. Ltd. 23; Factory 32
"Gibber" plains: S.A. 16, 194, 207
Gibson Desert, W.A. 150, 175
Giese, Harry 146, 147
Gladstone, Qld. 102
Glenrowan, Vic. 47
Gold Coast, Qld. 97, 101-102, 111-114
Golding, W. R., Mayor 102
Gold mining: New South Wales 76; Northern Territory 148; Queensland 99, 100, 104, 123, 132; Victoria 45; Western Australia 169, 173, 173-174, 188
Goodparla station, N.T. 138
Gorton, John Grey, Prime Minister 49-50, 63
Gosse, W. C. 214
Government 49-50, 73, 74
Great Artesian Basin 125
Great Australian Bight 174
Great Barrier Reef 99, 102-104, 116
Great Britain 84, 101, 118
Great Dividing Range, Vic., N.S.W., Qld. 15, 48, 99, 121
Great Sandy Desert, W.A. 150
Great Victoria Desert, W.A. 150
Green, Dr. Michael 208

ADDITIONAL REFERENCES

General: Alan Barnard, *The Simple Fleece;* David Beal and Donald Horne, *Southern Exposure;* Geoffrey Blainey, *Mines in the Spinifex;* Robin Boyd, *The Australian Ugliness;* Jeff Carter, *People of the Inland* and *The Life and Land of Central Australia;* Peter Coleman, editor, *Australian Civilization;* Robert B. Goodman and George Johnston, *The Australians;* The Grolier Society of Australia, *The Australian Encyclopedia;* Donald Horne, *The Lucky Country;* Elspeth Huxley, *Their Shining Eldorado;* Alex Kerr, *Australia's North-West;* Robin Smith, *The Red Centre.*

History: Ronald Anderson, *On the Sheep's Back;* Marjorie Barnard, *A History of Australia;* J. C. Beaglehole, *Exploration of the Pacific* and *The Journals of Capt. James Cook;* Bill Beatty, *A Treasury of Australian Folk Tales and Traditions;* Geoffrey Blainey, *The Tyranny of Distance;* Frank Clune, *Wild Colonial Boys;* David Collins, *An Account of the English Colony in New South Wales;* J. H. E. Crumpston, *The Inland Sea and the Great River;* J. M. Freeland, *The Australian Pub;* Ernestine Hill, *Water into Gold;* Hector Holthouse, *River of Gold;* Alan Moorehead, *Cooper's Creek, Gallipoli,* and *Rum Jungle;* Andrew Sharp, *The Discovery of Australia;* Charles Sturt, *Narrative of an Expedition into Central Australia.*

Flora and Fauna: Australian News and Information Bureau, *Bush Dwellers of Australia;* William J. Dakin, *The Great Barrier Reef;* Harry Frauca, *The Book of Australian Wildlife;* H. J. Frith, *Waterfowl in Australia;* Keith Gillett and Frank McNeill, *The Great Barrier Reef and Adjacent Isles;* Bernhard Grzimek, *Four-Legged Australians;* Francis Ratcliffe, *Flying Fox and Drifting Sand;* Vincent Serventy, *A Continent in Danger* and *Australia's Great Barrier Reef.*

Language: Sidney J. Baker, *The Australian Language;* Afferbeck Lauder, *Let Stalk Strine.*

Literature: Nino Culotta, *They're a Weird Mob;* Mrs. Aeneas Gunn, *We of the Never-Never;* Banjo Paterson, *The Man from Snowy River* and *The World of Banjo Paterson;* Olaf Ruhen, *Naked Under Capricorn;* Russell Ward, *Australian Ballads;* Patrick White, *The Tree of Man* and *Voss;* Judith Wright, editor, *A Book of Australian Verse.*

Art: Kym Bonython, *Modern Australian Painting and Sculpture;* Rex and Thea Rienits, *Early Artists of Australia;* Bernard Smith, *Australian Painting.*

Aborigines: Ronald M. Berndt, editor, *Australian Aboriginal Art;* Ronald M. and Catherine H. Berndt, *The First Australians* and *The World of the First Australians;* A. P. Elkin, *The Australian Aborigines.*

For additional reading on Australia, you may wish to refer to the following NATIONAL GEOGRAPHIC articles and to check the Cumulative Index for related material.

Beverley M. Bowie: "Off the Beaten Track of Empire (Prince Philip's Tour)," Nov., 1957. Norman Chaffer: "Australia's Amazing Bowerbirds," Dec., 1961. David Fleay: "Flight of the Platypuses," Oct., 1958; "Strange Animals of Australia," Sept., 1963. David H. Johnson: "The Incredible Kangaroo," Oct., 1955. Charles P. Mountford: "Earth's Most Primitive People: A Journey with the Aborigines of Central Australia," Jan., 1946; "Exploring Stone Age Arnhem Land," Dec., 1949; "Expedition to the Land of the Tiwi," Mar., 1956. T. C. Roughley: "Where Nature Runs Riot: On Australia's Great Barrier Reef," June, 1940; " 'Bounty' Descendants Live on Remote Norfolk Island," Oct., 1960. L. H. Smith: "Lyrebird, Australia's Meistersinger," June, 1955. Alan Villiers: "Australia. Part I: The West and South. Part II: The Settled East, the Barrier Reef, the Center," and "Australia on Maps — Old and New," Sept., 1963; " 'The Alice' in Australia's Wonderland," Feb., 1966. Howell Walker: "Facing War's Challenge 'Down Under,' " and "Making of an Anzac," Apr., 1942; "Cruise to Stone Age Arnhem Land," Sept., 1949; "The Making of a New Australia," Feb., 1956. Paul A. Zahl: "On Australia's Coral Ramparts," Jan., 1957.

Green Island, Great Barrier Reef 103, *116*
Griffin, Burley 63
Groote Eylandt, N.T. 47
Grounds, Roy 55
Gum trees 24, *48,* 100, *131, 187*
Gympie, Qld. 100

Hamersley Ranges, W.A. 151
Hamilton Downs station, N.T. 198
Hannan, Paddy 188
Happy Jacks Dam, Tumut River 49
Hawksbury River, N.S.W.: Oyster farm *93*
Hayman Island, Whitsunday group 103
Heavitree Gap, Macdonnell Ranges *211*
Hermannsburg Aboriginal Mission, N.T.: Residents *212*
Hermit crab *116*
Heron Island, Qld. 102-103
High Court of Australia 73
History 28, 46-47, 49-50, 75, 100; Exploration 10-11, 23, 24, 101; Settlement 69, 127; World War I 52, 145; World War II 80, 97, 121, 147, 148, 151
Hobart, Tas. 28, *40-41,* 51, 70
Hogg, Capt. Pearl 26
Holt, Harold 50
Holthouse, Hector 12, 97
Horse racing 12, 46, *58-59,* 135
Humpty Doo, N.T. 149
Hyde Park, Sydney *83*
Hydroelectric power 28; Tidal power 151; *see also* Snowy Mountains Hydro-electric Scheme

Iffley station, Qld. 126
Illawarra Range, N.S.W. *90*
Immigration 12, 23-24, 46, 50, 76, 100, 135, *181*
Indian Ocean 11, 150, 169
Industry 23, 28, 47, 72, 75, *90,* 98, 102, 170; *see also* Cattle; Fishing; Lumbering; Mining; Oil; Sheep; Sugar cane
Innisfail, Qld.: Canefields *118*
Iron ore production: Tasmania 28; Western Australia 150, 151-152, *152, 155, 161,* 170
Irrigation: Murray River valley 24-25, 28, *35;* Ord River 150, *156*
Ivanhoe Valley, W.A. *156*

Jacoby, Harry *145*
Jarrah trees 171
Jimboomba 51
Jungari, Victor *212*

Kalgoorlie, W.A. *188;* Gold mines 173-174, *175*
Kambalda, W.A.: Nickel deposit 152
Kanakas 100
Kangaroo paws, wild flower *184*
Kangaroos *4,* 72, *108,* 128, 176, *193,* 193, 195, 199, 200, *207*
Karri trees 171, *176*
Keenan, J. P. 26
Kelly, Ned 46-47
Kings Cross, Sydney 71, *80,* 84
Koalas 24, *108*

Kojonup, W.A. 51
Koolan Island, W.A.: Iron ore 150, 155
Kosciusko, Mount, N.S.W. 51, 64, 66
Kununurra, W.A. 150, 156
Kuri Bay, W.A.: Pearl farms 151, 159
Ku-ring-gai Chase, park, N.S.W. 72
Kwinana, W.A. 170

Lamshed, Max 22
Liebelt, J. L., 27
Light, Col. William 22-23
Lily, fringed *185*
Lindsay, Peter 25
Livistona mariae 197
Lizard, monitor 148
Lone Pine Sanctuary, Brisbane *108*
Lorikeets *108*
Lubbock, Frank 174
Lumbering 171, 176

MacArthur, Gen. Douglas 97-98
Macdonnell Ranges, N.T. 196-197, *211*
McEwen, John, Deputy Prime Minister *63*
Mair, Fritz 103
Manly Beach, Sydney *88-89*
Manly Surf Life Saving Club 72
Maps: Population density *10;* Route *22, 46, 70, 98, 122, 146, 170, 194;* Snowy Mountains Hydro-electric Scheme *51*
Marineland of Australia, Surfers Paradise *114*
Mariposa 9-12
Maritime Services Board 70
Marsupials: Dibbler 172, *175;* Kangaroos 72, *108,* 128, 176, *193,* 193, 195, 197, 199, *207;* Koalas 24, *108;* Tasmanian wolf *25,* 27
Mary River, Qld. 100
Melbourne, Vic. 11, 21, 28, *45,* 45-47, 48, 64, 93; Amphitheater *60;* Arts center *55;* Culture 55, 60; History 45-46; Population 47, 55; Shopping district *52;* University 56
Melbourne Cup: Parade *58-59;* Spectators *13*
Melville Island, N.T.: Aboriginal settlement 128, *141-142,* 146-147
Menindee Lake, N.S.W. 38
Menzies, Sir Robert 56
Merino sheep *4, 95, 207*
Meter Maid: Surfers Paradise 97
Middle Harbour, Sydney 70
Mildura, Vic. 24-25, 49; Arts Center 28
Millen, Andrew 170
Mining 26-27, *37,* 47, 127, *135,* 161; Gold 45, 99, 100, 104, 123, 132, 148, 173-174, 188; Iron ore 28, 150, 151-152, *152, 155,* 161; Opals 194, *202*
Moncrieff, Suzie 178
Monday Club: Melbourne *55*
Moondara, lake, Qld. 127
Moonie, Qld. 97
Moore, Warren 72
Morecombe, M.K. 172
Mount Goldsworthy, W.A. 151, 161
Mount Isa, Qld. 127, *128, 135*
Mount Lofty Ranges, S.A. 24
Mouse, freckled marsupial 172, *175*
Mundaring reservoir, W.A. *188*

Murray, Jock 171
Murray 1 power station 49
Murray 2 power station 49, *64*
Murray River 24, 49, *51,* 193; Steamers 26, *48*
Murrumbidgee River, N.S.W. 49, 51
Myer, Sidney Music Bowl 60

Nash, James 100
National emblem *187*
National Gallery of Victoria, Melbourne: Reception hall *55*
National Geographic Society: Melville Island expedition 147
Natural gas 47, 162
Naustitermes triodiae 137
Neale, John 24
New South Wales: Art Gallery, Sydney 74; Capital *see* Sydney; Economy 72; Industry 72, 75; Mining 26-27, *37;* Oyster farming 93; Parks 72; Sheep raising 75-76, *95;* Wildlife 72
Newman, Mount, W.A. *161*
Nickel deposit: Kambalda 152
Norman River, Qld. *15,* 123-124, 132
Normanton, Qld. 124, 125, *132;* Council Chambers *121, 132;* Windmill 128
North Shore, Sydney 71, 78
Northern Territory 128, 138, 145-149, 195-200; Aboriginal settlements *141-142,* 146-147, 199-200, *212;* Capital *see* Darwin; Wildlife 148, 199, 200
Nossal, Dr. Gustav 56
Nullarbor Plain, S.A.-W.A. 175-176
Nuytsia 186

Oil 47, 97, 152; Drilling rig *162*
O'Keefe, J. T. 47
Olga, Mount, N.T. *214*
Oliphant, Sir Mark 50
Opal mining 194, *202*
Orchards 35
Ord River Irrigation Scheme 150, *156*
Outback 99, 121-128, 193-200
Oyster farming: New South Wales 93
Oysters 102

Paddington, Sydney *80*
Palm Valley, N.T. *16*
Palmer River, Qld.: Gold rush 99, 104
Papunya Aboriginal Reserve, N.T. 199-200, 212
Parks 24, 72; Wildlife sanctuaries *108*
Parliament 49-50, 74
Parliament House, Canberra 63
Parliament House, Melbourne *45*
Pasco Island, W.A. 152
Pearling industry 151, 159, 165
Perth, W.A. 149, 150, 169, *170,* 170, 173, *181;* History 178; Parks 170-171; People *178*
Phillip, Arthur, Governor 69
Pickering, Kevin R. 25
Pitjantjara tribe 200, 214
Platypus, duckbill *4*
Poinciana tree *165*
Point Piper, Sydney 69
Pollnitz, Percy F. 24
Population *10,* 10, 11, 12, 22, 47, 50, 55, 69, 71, 84, 106, 148, 178, 196

Porpoises *114*
Port Arthur, Tas.: Penal colony 28, 74;
  Ruins *40-41*
Port Augusta, S.A. 176, 193; Hospital *208*
Port Hedland, W.A. 151, *161*
Port Jackson (Sydney Harbour) 10, 11,
  69
Port Kembla, N.S.W. 90
Port Latta, Tas. 28
"Port of Pearls" *see* Broome, W.A.
Port Phillip, Melbourne 45
Port Pirie, S.A. 21, 176
Prenzel, Don *37-38*
Python, tree 147, 148

Rabbits 75-76
Railways 149, 161, 169, 174, 175, 176,
  193, 196, 211
Rainfall 18, 121-123, 132
Raisin, Mrs. Beryl 124
Rapley, King *37-38*
Resort areas: Alice Springs 196-197;
  Cairns 104; Esperance 172; Gold
  Coast 97, 101,102, *111-114;* Great
  Barrier Reef 102-103; Menindee
  Lake *38;* Mount Kosciusko area 66;
  Whitsunday islands 103
Road trains 127-128, *211*
Royal Arcade, Melbourne *52*
Royal Flying Doctor Service 27, 197,
  208
Ruhen, Olaf 72
Rushcutters Bay, Sydney 69

Sailboats: Sydney Harbour *78, 86, 87*
Sailing 70, *78,* 86-87
Sailmaker: Hobart *41*
St. George's Terrace, Perth 169
St. Mary's Convent School, Broome *159*
St. Patrick's Cathedral, Melbourne *45*
St. Vincent, Gulf of 23
Savage River, Tas. 28
Sawer, Derek 47
School of the Air 27, 123, 198, 207;
  Teacher *37*
Selwyn Range, Qld. *135*
Sheep *4, 18-19, 95, 207;* Sheep
  station 75-76, *207*
Sipponen, Ensio *64*
Skiing *66*
Snake Bay, N.T. *147*
Snowy Mountains, N.S.W.-Vic *15*
Snowy Mountains Hydro-electric
  Scheme 46, 48-49, *64,* 66, 101; Map
  51; Power station *64*
Soccer *32*
South Australia 21-24, 193-195; Capital
  see Adelaide; History 22-23, 194;
  Industry 23; Mining 23, *202;* Parks
  24; Wine-making *21,* 24
South Australian Housing Trust 23-24
Southern Hemisphere 10, *45*

Space tracking station: Carnarvon 152,
  166
Spencer Gulf 21
Spice Islands, Indonesia 11, 151
Spinifex grass 122, *162*
Sports 6, *32, 38;* Cricket *30;*
  Sailing 70, *78,* 86-87; Skiing 66;
  Soccer *32;* Surfing *89, 104, 113;*
  Tennis, *7, 31; see also* Horse racing
Stefanapoulos family *202*
Steel mills: Port Kembla *90*
Stirling Range 186
Stromb, red-mouthed *116*
Stromlo, Mount, N.S.W. 52
Stuart Highway, N.T. 128, *211*
Stubbs, Capt. Cheslyn *183*
Sturt, Charles 24, 186
Sturt Highway, S.A. 24
Sturt's desert pea *186*
Sugar cane: Queensland 100-101;
  Harvest *118*
Sunraysia District Citrus Cooperative
  Society, Ltd. 25
Surf Life Saving Association of
  Australia: Carnival *88*
Surfers Paradise, Qld. 97, 101-102;
  Marineland *114;* Meter Maid *97;*
Surfing *89, 104, 113*
Swan River, W.A. 170
Sydney 9-12, 69-74, 78-80, *83, 84, 88,*
  93, 97, 148; Architecture 71; Beaches
  71-72, 88-89; Fountains 71, *80;*
  History 69, *72;* Parks 74, *83;* Popula-
  tion 11, 69, 71; Port facilities 70;
  Shipping 70-71; Suburbs 76
Sydney Harbour 11, *69, 78,* 86-87;
  Harbour Bridge 12, 78
Sydney-Hobart yacht race 70, 86-87
Sydney Opera House 69, 71, *78*

Tan, Josephine *137*
Tasmania 11; Agriculture *27, 42;*
  Capital *see* Hobart; Exports 27, 40;
  History 28; Mining 28
Tasmanian wolf *25,* 27
Tasman Peninsula, Tas. *40*
Tennis *7, 31*
Termite mounds: Northern Territory
  128, *137*
Thompson, Brian *4,* 75-76, *95*
Thylacinus cynocephalus (Tasmanian
  wolf) *25,* 27
Thysanotus 185
Tiwi tribesmen *141-142,* 146-147
Todd, Charles and Alice 196
Todd River, Alice Springs *211*
Tom Price, Mount, W.A. 151
Trans-Australian Railway 174-176
Transcontinental telegraph 193, 196
Transportation: Camels *149,* 150; Rail-
  ways 149, 161, 174-176, 196; Road
  trains 127, *211;* Steamers 26, 48
Toowoomba, Qld. 99
Tullo, Norma 55
Tweed Heads, N.S.W. 114

Tumut 2 power station *64*
Tumut River, N.S.W. 49, *51*

U. S. Navy communications base:
  Exmouth Gulf 152
University of Melbourne: Commence-
  ment *56;* Laboratory *56*
University of Queensland 104

Van Diemen's Land (Tasmania) 28, 193
Victoria 24; Capital *see* Melbourne;
  Irrigation 25, 28, 35
Victoria Racing Club: Members *58*
Victory Downs, S.A. 195
Vineyards *21, 35, 55*
Volunteer Coastal Patrol 70

Walker, Howell 27
Wallaby 25
War Memorial, Canberra *see*
  Australian War Memorial
Waratah *84*
Waratah Festival: Sydney *84*
Warrie station, N.S.W. 75-76, *95*
Water buffalo 128, *138*
Water supply 15, 47-49, 50, 123, 194,
  195; Artesian basins 125, 128, *204,*
Wattle, tree *187*
Weipa, Qld. 102
Westbrook, Eric 55
Western Australia 149-152, 169-175;
  Agriculture *18-19, 150, 156,* 171,
  172, *191;* Area 145; Capital *see* Perth;
  Development 151-152; Flora 172,
  175, *184-187;* Industry 170; Mineral
  resources 150, 151-152, 162, 170;
  Mining *152, 155,* 173-174, 188; Lum-
  bering 171; Population *178;* Terrain
  149-150
Weatherburn, Charles 71
Welbourn Hill, N.T. 195
Whaling: Western Australia 171, *183*
Whicker, P. W. 23
"White Australia Policy" 50, 100
Whitsunday group, islands, Qld. 103
Whyalla, S.A. 47
William Street, Sydney *80*
Willis, Sam *188*
Windmill *128*
Wine-making *20,* 24
Wondoola station, Qld. 126
Wool production 19, 47, 75
Woomera, S.A. 193
Woomera 142, 193, *196*
Wrotham Park station, Qld. *131*

Yarra River, Vic. 45

Zebu 127
Zinc Corporation Ltd. 27

Composition by National Geographic's Phototypographic Division, Herman J.A.C.
Arens, Director; John E. McConnell, Manager. Printed and bound by Fawcett-Haynes
Printing Corp., Rockville, Md. Color separations by Lanman Engraving Co., Alexandria,
Va.; Beck Engraving Co., Philadelphia, Pa.; Graphic Color Plate, Inc., Stamford, Conn.;
and Stevenson Photocolor, Inc., Cincinnati, Ohio.